MALTA

Sean Sheehan

MARSHALL CAVENDISH
New York • London • Sydney

Reference edition reprinted 2000 by
Marshall Cavendish Corporation
99 White Plains Road
Tarrytown
New York 10591

© Times Media Private Limited 2000

Originated and designed by
Times Books International, an imprint of
Times Media Private Limited, a member of the
Times Publishing Group

Printed in Singapore

Library of Congress Cataloging-in-Publication Data:

Sheehan, Sean, 1951–
    Malta / Sean Sheehan.
        p. cm. — (Cultures of the world)
    Includes bibliographical references and index.
    ISBN 0-7614-0993-9 (lib. bdg.)
    1. Malta—Civilization—Juvenile literature. I. Title.
II. Series.

DG989.7 .S54 2000
945.8'5—dc21   99-053436
                   CIP
                   AC

INTRODUCTION

MALTA, A SMALL ARCHIPELAGO in the center of the Mediterranean, has attracted foreign cultures from time immemorial, but it is not only its megalithic temples that bear testimony to more than 6,000 years of human history. Beginning with ancient, unknown migrants from neighboring lands in the Mediterranean, and continuing apace with the crowd of tourists that now invade the islands every year, Malta has remarkably managed to preserve its culture.

This is borne out by the Maltese language, which continues to thrive among a people that number well below half a million. The durability of its national tongue is just one example of Malta's resilience—this book introduces the reader to many other aspects of this small European culture that maintains its independence with dignity and fortitude. As Europe grows closer together, economically and politically, Malta serves to show how a minority culture can avoid becoming an endangered one.

CONTENTS

Buses are the main form of public transportation in Malta.

CONTENTS

A guard at Fort St. Elmo.

GEOGRAPHY

MALTA CONSISTS OF THREE MAIN ISLANDS—the island of Malta itself, the smaller island of Gozo, and the tiny Comino. Cominotto, Filfla, and St. Paul's Islands are large rocks that help make up the Maltese archipelago. All the islands lie midway between Gibraltar, at the western end of the Mediterranean Sea, and Lebanon at the eastern end. To the north lies the island of Sicily, 58 miles (93 km) away, while 220 miles (354 km) to the south lies Tripoli, the seaport capital of Libya. Malta is located in the center of the Mediterranean, midway between Europe and North Africa.

The largest island, Malta, is 17 miles (27 km) long and nine miles (14 km) wide and covers an area of 95 square miles (246 square km). Gozo is only nine miles (14 km) long by five miles (eight km) wide, with an area of 26 square miles (67 square km), while Comino has an area of only one square mile (2.6 square km). A channel of water three miles (five km) wide separates Malta and Gozo, and Comino lies between them.

The islands of Malta cover an area of 122 square miles (316 square km).

Opposite: **The "Azure Window," an unusual natural rock formation on the western coast of Gozo.**

Left: **Marfa Ridge on Malta island and in the background, Comino island across the South Comino Channel.**

TERRAIN

The three main islands are mostly composed of limestone and rise to a maximum height of just over 829 feet (253 m) at the Dingli Cliffs in the southwest of Malta island. However, the land is not as flat as this might suggest as there are lots of escarpments, or steep slopes at the edge of an area of level ground that drop into a narrow valley.

One of the most prominent escarpments is the Mdina-Verdala Ridge, where the Dingli Cliffs are situated. To the north of the ridge, separated by small hills, is an array of narrow valleys that make their way down to the coast. These lower-lying areas have good alluvial soils and are cultivated with the help of irrigation.

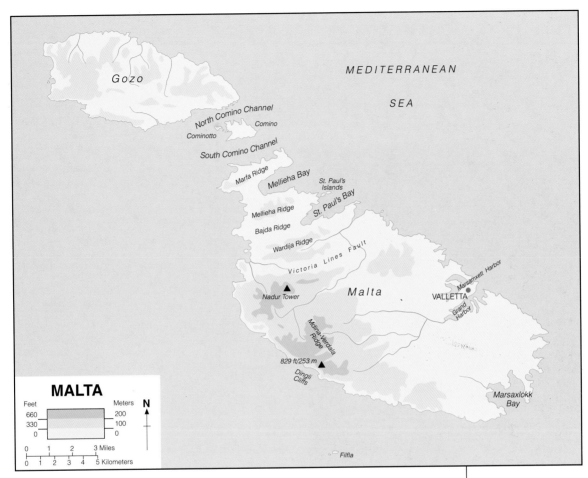

Malta's terrain is mostly rocky and sparse, devoid of mountains and rivers and with little vegetation, although there are many small fields enclosed by stone walls. Between February and March, Malta is briefly transformed into myriads of colors when tulips, crocuses, and other flowers brighten up the otherwise barren countryside. The island of Gozo, thanks to its clayey soil, has a more verdant landscape.

The coastlines of the main islands are well indented and there are countless small harbors, creeks, bays, and sandy coves. The Grand Harbor in Valletta is a natural deep-water harbor 80 feet (24 m) deep and has been of great economic as well as strategic importance for thousands of years. The total length of the shoreline around Malta island is 84 miles (135 km), and 27 miles (43 km) around Gozo.

FAUNA AND FLORA

Malta does not have a great variety of wildlife. The shortage of water combined with the poor quality of the soil has resulted in the Mediterranean shrub being the only natural vegetation. The mammals that are able to survive are mostly small animals, such as hedgehogs, weasels, and shrews. Resident birds include the Manx and Cory's shearwaters, the blue rock thrush, and the Sardinian warbler. During spring and autumn, Malta is visited by countless thousands of migrating birds, but the shooting of these birds has become a popular leisure activity for some Maltese.

The Judas tree (*Cercis siliquastrum*) is common. It derives its name from the legend that this was the tree from which Judas Iscariot, an apostle of Christ, hanged himself after betraying Jesus. At one time, oak trees covered the islands, but most have long since been cut down. Only a few small pockets of these indigenous trees remain.

What has survived in more plentiful numbers is the carob or algarroba (*Ceratonia siliqua*), also known as the locust tree, which derives its name from a Biblical legend associated with both John the Baptist and the Prodigal Son. The pods are edible, and although now used mainly to feed cattle, they were once a source of food for hungry peasants. The juice from the pods was also used to make drinks and syrups. Other trees that are able to survive Malta's hot and dry climate include the fig, the sweet bay, and the almond.

Date palms, imported from North Africa, are a common sight. Also found on Malta are orange trees, which were also introduced to the islands. Malta has over 600 species of wildflowers.

Opposite: **Bright orange-colored flowers cover a field.**

FLOWERS

Malta is not a place usually associated with colorful flowers. This is partly because the flowering season lasts only a couple of months and partly because the soil and the climate do not encourage a rich variety of plants. What does flourish is a giant clover, the sulla, which produces a purple-colored flower. Because farmers use it as a fodder crop, its growth is encouraged.

Shrubs that flower are cultivated for ornamental purposes along roads and at other public places. These include the pink-and-white oleander, the orange-colored lantana, the geranium, and the bougainvillea. Some of these shrubs are also nurtured in pots by families who like to add some color to the exterior of their homes by placing painted or pottery containers against an outside wall. Apartment-dwellers often like to cultivate flowering shrubs that hang down from their balconies. Even in very arid areas, the ubiquitous prickly pear (*opuntia*), a type of cactus, bears a yellow flower in autumn.

CLIMATE

Summers in Malta are long, hot, and dry. Winters are mild and snowfall is unknown. Although the average yearly rainfall is 20 inches (51 cm), it rarely rains during the summer months. The average temperature between April and October is 77°F (25°C), although temperatures may rise to 96°F (36°C). In the winter months, from November to March, the average temperature is 54°F (12°C).

This typical Mediterranean combination of a long and hot summer with a dry and mild winter is ideal for attracting tourists from colder climates. Not surprisingly, Malta is very popular with visitors all year around. Moreover, because no place in Malta is more than a few

THE MALTESE FALCON AND THE SQUIRTING CUCUMBER

The famous Maltese falcon, the title of one of Hollywood's most memorable black-and-white movies, is the Mediterranean peregrine falcon. It used to nest under cliffs on Gozo island, but sadly became a protected species too late to save it from extinction in the mid-1980s. The same fate befell the Mediterranean sea eagle—another victim of the peculiar "hobby" of killing birds that is still widely practiced in Malta.

The squirting cucumber, or *faqqus il-hmir* ("FAT-ous ill-hmeer"), may not be as well-known as the Maltese falcon, but it is thriving and is in no danger of extinction, thanks perhaps to its peculiar form of propagation. The seeds of most plants are usually spread by bees, animals, or the wind, but the *faqqus il-hmir* is able to eject its seeds with enough force to propel them a distance away. The seeds are formed in a liquid-filled fruit that dramatically explodes when ripe, thus spreading the seeds. The *faqqus il-hmir* is a very common plant in Malta and grows on wasteland.

miles from the sea, sea breezes help moderate the heat of the summer months. The best known of these cooling winds is the *gregale* ("grey-GAH-lay"), which blows in from high altitudes in southern Italy and Sicily. The *gregale* can last up to three days and is feared by fishermen because of its ability to whip up waves and endanger small craft.

In early summer and again at the end of the summer, a warm and sultry wind blows in from the Sahara Desert in Africa. Called the *scirocco* ("shi-ROCK-o"), some people believe the wind affects their temperament, causing them to become annoyed by small matters that would not normally bother them.

Opposite: **The fertile Ramla Valley in Gozo.**

A LAND WITHOUT RIVERS

Malta has no rivers. In the past this meant complete dependence on water from wells. Small, privately-owned windmills are a common sight in the countryside, where they are used to power wells to irrigate farm land. The government has built many reservoirs, and there are also a number of desalination plants, which extract salt from sea water before it is pumped into a reservoir.

Water is also pumped up from natural underground hollows in the rock where rainwater that has percolated through the soil collects. In Malta the water table is usually found some 30 to 60 feet (nine to 18 m) below the surface. Drilling a well to reach the water is no longer a problem with modern technology. Desalination plants account for over 60% of the water used on the island and, although expensive, has relieved the shortage of fresh water.

Buses connect the main urban centers in Malta to outlying villages along a 800-mile (1,288-km) network of roads.

URBAN CENTERS

Although Valletta is the capital of Malta, it is not the largest town. Less than 10,000 people live in Valletta, compared to the towns of Birkirkara and Qormi, which have more than twice as many people. Over 13,000 people live in Sliema, a prosperous middle-class district on Malta island. Sliema, situated close to Valletta, is home to the fashionable Tower Road, where boutiques and other upscale shops adjoin blocks of luxurious apartments.

The original capital of Malta was Mdina, an inland town. The site of this fortified city was well chosen—a high precipice on a ridge that was easy to defend. But when the Knights of St. John arrived in the 16th century,

LIFE IN THE SEA

The Mediterranean Sea has some of the most polluted waters in the world and this has affected the diversity of the sea life around Malta. There are several varieties of mackerel as well as red mullet, bass, and skate. Local fish popular in restaurants and Maltese kitchens include *dentici* ("den-TEE-chee"), *lampuka* ("lam-POO-ka"), and *pixxixspad* ("pish-SHISH-pad").

The small fishing industry uses traditional Maltese fishing boats, called *luzzijiet* ("LUT-tsie-yiet"), which are a familiar sight at small harbors around Malta and Gozo. As in other Mediterranean cultures, there is a lively tradition of painting boats in bright colors and adding an image of a large eye on either side of the prow.

they preferred a base closer to the coast. When the Great Siege of 1565 ended, the Knights committed themselves to making Malta their permanent home and built a new capital that could hold a commanding position over the main harbor. The capital was named after the leader of the Knights, the Grand Master Jean Parisot de la Valette, who had led them to their great victory over the Turks.

The largest town in Gozo is Victoria. Its original name, and one by which it is sometimes still identified, is Rabat (meaning "the town"), but this was changed by the British in 1897 to commemorate Queen Victoria. Unlike many other countries colonized by the British, the Maltese have not felt the need to assert their independence by removing linguistic markers of imperial rule.

Valletta, the capital of Malta, is the seat of government as well as the country's cultural center.

7 TA GUNJU 1919

HISTORY

MALTA HAS JUSTLY BEEN LABELED THE CRADLE of Mediterranean culture because of its many megaliths that date back to the dawn of European civilization. More generally, the history of Malta can be seen to encapsulate European history as a whole. It began with the first arrival of nomadic peoples from Sicily in the north some 7,000 years ago. The Neolithic cave-dwellers who built the megaliths were followed by a Bronze Age society.

Then came a succession of more powerful cultures—Carthaginians, Romans, Arabs, Normans, the Knights of St. John, the French, and then the British at the turn of the 19th century. Finally, the Maltese gained their independence in 1964.

Opposite: **A memorial in Palace Square in Valletta commemorates the 1919 riots that led to greater self-government for the Maltese under British rule.**

Left: **The Tarxien temples southeast of Valletta are among the best preserved Neolithic structures in Malta.**

TEMPLE BUILDERS

The ancient Greeks, impressed by the sweet product of the bees on Malta, named the islands Melita *("honey").*

The earliest inhabitants were Stone Age people who are thought to have first arrived in Malta around 5000 B.C. Although they lacked knowledge of metals, they used their expertise with stone to leave a permanent reminder of their presence on Malta. Around the same time that the Egyptians first began building pyramids, the Neolithic Maltese began constructing impressive megalithic temples on Gozo and Malta.

Some of the most famous temples, such as the Tarxien ("tar-SHEEN") temple and the Hypogeum of Hal Saflieni, were only discovered by accident early in the 20th century. Tarxien was uncovered when a farmer plowing his field kept blunting his plow on large stones just under the soil.

KEY DATES IN MALTA'S HISTORY

Before 5000 B.C.	First settlement by people, probably arriving from the north
Around 3200 B.C.	The great megalithic temples are built
A.D. 60	The shipwrecked St. Paul arrives on the island and Christianity is introduced
870	Malta is conquered by the Arabs
1090	Normans invade Malta
1530	The Order of St. John first arrives
1565	The Great Siege
1798	France captures Malta
1800	British rule begins
1921	First Maltese government, under British control
1964	Malta becomes an independent state
1974	Malta becomes a republic

Later, excavations revealed a temple complex and important prehistoric works of art. The Hypogeum, a vast underground chamber cut from rock and later used as a burial chamber, was discovered by a builder working on the foundations for a house he was building.

PHOENICIANS AND CARTHAGINIANS

The influence of the Phoenicians and the Carthaginians was felt from around 1500 B.C. to 216 B.C. The Phoenicians, a Bronze Age maritime power based in what is now Lebanon in the eastern Mediterranean, used Malta as a staging post as they sailed from one end of the Mediterranean to the other. They also established a colony at Carthage, in what is now Tunisia in North Africa. The Carthaginians developed their own power base after Phoenicia declined in importance.

The Phoenicians dominated trade in the Mediterranean some 3,000 years ago. Tombs have been uncovered in Malta, suggesting that some Phoenicians settled on the islands.

A small number of Phoenician inscriptions have been found in Malta and being a Semitic language it was believed for a long time that Maltese was Phoenician in origin. The Carthaginians also used Malta as a base, and although there is little archeological evidence of their presence, their influence lives on in the popular Maltese name, Nibblu, which is a shortened form of Hannibal, the most famous Carthaginian in history. After a fierce struggle against the power of Rome, Carthage was finally destroyed. For Malta this heralded a long period of rule under the Romans.

THE ROMANS

Rome, which held undisputed power over the entire Mediterranean region, paid little attention to Malta even though the islands remained under Roman influence for some 800 years. The Romans first arrived during the Second Punic War (218–201 B.C.) between Rome and Carthage, and Malta fell under the responsibility of the Roman governor of Sicily.

In A.D. 60 a ship heading for Rome was shipwrecked

Malta became an outpost of the Roman Empire after the Carthaginians were defeated in the Second Punic War.

off the coast of Malta. There were well over 200 passengers on board. One of them, St. Paul, remained on the island for three months and converted the Roman governor, Publius. This is how Christianity is believed to have come to Malta, which was one of the earliest Roman colonies to be Christianized. Today, the annual celebration of his shipwreck is still an important event. If the tradition is true, then the Maltese were one of the first non-Jewish people to convert to the new religion.

THE ARABS

The islands of Malta were conquered by the Arabs in A.D. 870. The new invaders would retain control until the arrival of the Normans 220 years later. Not a great deal is known about how Malta was governed during this period because the conquerors regarded these small islands as only a tiny part of a vast area of influence that spread from Spain in the west, across the Mediterranean and including Sicily, to the Indus River in the east.

Malta, as in the days of Roman rule, was only a province of Sicily. Nevertheless, the short period of Arab conquest had a lasting effect on the language that would develop into the Maltese that is spoken today. The introduction to Malta of citrus fruits and cotton is also attributed to the Arabs. The Arabs built their fortified capital, which they named Mdina, on the site of the old Roman capital.

Although they introduced their language to the islanders, they did not convert the people to Islam and so Christianity retained its influence over the lives of the people of Malta.

During Arab rule, the walled city of Mdina was the capital of Malta.

THE NORMANS

The Normans, a mixed race of people from Normandy in France, conquered large parts of the Mediterranean in the 11th century, including Sicily. In 1090 they arrived from Sicily and began to displace the Arabs as rulers of Malta. The Arabs living on Malta did not resist the Normans by force, and Muslims continued to live there as before. It was not until 1224 that the Muslims were expelled from the islands.

Unlike the Romans, the various Norman rulers who governed Malta failed to contain the major problem of marauding pirates from North Africa. Known as corsairs, the pirates found Malta to be a useful watering hole and base for mounting attacks on passing shipping. As a result, Malta never endeared itself to the European powers, especially after a raid in 1525 led to 400 persons of various ranks and nationalities being captured and either enslaved or held for ransom. By this time, Malta had passed into the hands of the Spanish emperor, Charles V, and he offered it to the Knights of St. John, who were anxiously looking for a new home.

In 1530 Charles V granted Malta to the homeless Knights of St. John, who then ruled the islands for over 250 years.

THE ORDER OF ST. JOHN

The year 1530 is very significant in Malta's history because this was when the Knights of the Order of St. John first arrived on the islands. The Order exercised political and economic control over the islands. The police, the legal system, and even the water supply were all controlled by the Order, and all the key positions in the administration of Malta were held by

ASSEDIO E BATTERIA DI S.ELMO ADI 27 MAGGIO 1565

Knights. The local population, which numbered around 12,000 in 1530, had little contact with the Knights, but they were subject to them, and thanks to the Order's control of the police and military garrisons, the population had little choice but to accept their authority.

A tapestry depicting the Great Siege of 1565. The anniversary of the ending of the siege on September 8 is one of the most important public holidays in Malta.

THE GREAT SIEGE

The Knights had little interest in an inland capital like Mdina so they set about building new bases on the coast. In May 1565 a huge fleet of Turkish ships with 40,000 men arrived, aiming to completely destroy the Knights. It took them a month to take Fort St. Elmo, but the Knights in Fort St. Angelo managed to hold out against a total surrender of the island. In September, when Christian reinforcements began to arrive, the Turks sailed away and the Great Siege was over. The Great Siege has entered Maltese history as one of the nation's great defining moments. The Knights' Grand Master, Jean Parisot de la Valette, survived the siege with just 600 men, while the leader of the Ottomans, Dragut, died in the fighting.

THE KNIGHTS OF ST. JOHN

The Order of St. John was first established in the late 11th century as the Hospitalers, a religious grouping of monks who set out to provide medical care for Christian pilgrims to the Holy Land. However, the Holy Land is also holy to Islam, and this brought the pilgrims into conflict with the Arabs and created a need for a military force capable of protecting the pilgrims. In this way, the Hospitalers evolved into an order of Christian Knights, drawn from the aristocratic families of Europe, who were committed to vows of celibacy, poverty, and obedience to their Grand Master. As Islam grew more powerful, the Knights were expelled from the Holy Land. They established a base on the island of Rhodes, off the coast of Greece. From there they could sail out to attack the enemy.

The Knights became pirates in their own way, taking every opportunity to attack Turkish merchants and rob their ships. The advance of Islam, driven by the Ottoman Empire, led to the expulsion of the Knights from Rhodes. After eight years of wandering around Europe seeking a home, they were granted the island of Malta in 1530.

The Grand Master, the most important rank in the Order, was the official head of the Knights. The Knights adopted the distinctive eight-pointed cross, the Maltese Cross, as their emblem. Each of the eight points of the cross represents one of the beatitudes given in Christ's sermon on the Mount, while the four main sections represent the Christian virtues of fortitude, justice, temperance, and prudence.

AFTER THE SIEGE

The Knights were determined to secure their island home against any future attack so work soon began on the building of Valletta. The town took five years to complete, gave the Knights a secure home for more than 200 years, and heralded an age of prosperity for Malta. By the mid-18th century, however, the Turkish Ottoman Empire was in decline and no longer posed a threat. The rule of the Knights came to an end in 1798 when Napoleon Bonaparte of France captured Malta and confiscated all their land and property. The revolutionary and anticlerical French army also abolished the Maltese nobility.

But by attacking the Church, the French made many enemies. When Napoleon set off for Egypt he left only a small force behind. When the Maltese rose in rebellion, the French were taken by surprise. They managed to hold out in Valletta until 1800 but finally surrendered and Malta fell into the hands of France's enemy at the time, the British.

BRITISH RULE

At first the British did not realize the strategic importance of their new acquisition, but in time they grew to appreciate the usefulness of controlling a small group of islands in the middle of the Mediterranean, especially after the opening of the Suez Canal in 1869.

After World War I, popular demonstrations calling for a greater say by the Maltese in the running of their country were held. In 1919 four Maltese were shot dead by British troops during a demonstration. Later the same year, the British announced plans to draw up a more liberal constitution. The new constitution left power over important matters such as defense and immigration in the hands of the British, but also created a Maltese government with an elected assembly to govern many other aspects of life. This system worked well until 1933, when the British suspended the Maltese government because it disapproved of its attempts to reintroduce Italian as the language of instruction in schools, instead of English. For the next 14 years, the Maltese government remained suspended.

A war cemetery in Malta commemorates members of the British armed forces who died during World War I.

Above: **The citation of April 1942 from George VI of England, when Malta received Britain's highest possible civilian award for exceptional courage—the George Cross. This honor was never before—or since—awarded to an entire country.**

Right: **Despite heavy bombing by German forces during World War II, Malta managed to hold out.**

WORLD WAR II

The strategic importance of Malta in any struggle for control of the Mediterranean became clearly obvious in World War II. Several German generals called for an invasion of the island because as long as it remained in British hands, enemy planes and submarines would be able to use it as a base. This would allow the British to attack the German convoys that were supplying their troops in the war in North Africa.

Adolf Hitler, however, preferred to launch an aerial attack and planned to bomb and starve Malta into submission by subjecting it to a second great siege. The island became one of the most heavily bombed targets during World War II. In two months in 1942, for example, more bombs were dropped on Malta than on the whole of London in a year. Many families moved to Gozo, where there was only a single small runway to attract the attention of enemy planes.

As essential supplies dwindled, it seemed almost certain that Malta would be forced to surrender. Everything came to depend on a convoy of 14 supply ships, escorted by battleships, aircraft carriers, cruisers, and destroyers, that set out on a final rescue mission in 1942. The convoy was an easy target for enemy planes and submarines, and the attempt to reach Malta became a dramatic journey through a corridor of bombs and torpedoes. When the *Ohio*, the first of the five supply ships that survived, was finally towed into the Grand Harbor, it was met by cheering crowds and tears of relief.

The Grand Harbor today. In 1942 a convoy of Allied ships carrying essential supplies sailed into the harbor and saved Malta from having to surrender to the Germans.

INDEPENDENCE

In the first general election after World War II, Malta gained its first Labor government. In 1955 Dominic Mintoff became the leader of the Labor Party. A charismatic and controversial politician, Mintoff led Malta's demands for full independence from Britain, which was finally achieved in 1964. The main difficulties facing the country were economic, a major

A FAMOUS FACE OF MALTA

Dominic (Dom) Mintoff was born in 1916 into a poor family and at a time when Malta, as just one of Britain's many overseas territories, had very little control over its own affairs. He trained as a civil engineer but became more interested in politics. He helped organize the Labor Party's first electoral victory in 1947 before going on to become the leader of the party. He was prime minister four times before finally stepping down in 1984.

Dom Mintoff became the most well-known Maltese politician internationally, due mainly to his relationship with Britain. At one stage, Mintoff was so pro-British that he suggested Malta should become an integral part of the United Kingdom itself. When this was rejected by Britain, his own position changed and he later led the demands for full independence.

Dom Mintoff is equally famous for his battles with the Catholic Church in Malta. He dared to openly criticize the Church for its authoritarianism and for its great wealth. He attempted to confiscate Church property and limit the political influence of priests. As a socialist, he struggled to improve the quality of life for the ordinary citizens of Malta, and in this respect, he achieved a great deal. Many important improvements, such as the introduction of free higher education, were due to his efforts. He is still revered by many Maltese. No other politician, before or since his time, has achieved so much for Malta.

setback being Britain's decision to cut its own defense budget by abandoning expensive overseas bases. In Malta, where the British employed about one in five of Malta's working population in its dockyards, this forced the country to look to its own future. In 1979 the British military base in Malta was finally closed, and the last of the British forces sailed away from the islands for the last time. Malta was now truly independent and entirely responsible for its own affairs.

In the same year, the first overtures were made to the European Economic Community (now the Economic Union), and in 1990 a formal application to join the EU was submitted.

MODERN-DAY KNIGHTS

Two hundred years after their expulsion from Malta by Napoleon's troops, the Knights of St. John made a triumphant return when they were granted a 99-year lease on Fort St. Angelo in 1998. The fort was the scene of their greatest victory in 1565, when some 600 Knights and 8,000 Maltese soldiers stemmed the tide of Muslim expansionism by successfully holding out against 40,000 Turks and their armada of 300 ships.

The Order of the Knights, now some 10,000 strong, has reverted to its original mission of caring for the sick and promoting the Catholic faith. Members, who continue to take vows of poverty, chastity, and obedience, maintain hospitals and aid missions in various parts of the world. The Order, now based in Rome, enjoys observer status at the United Nations and issues its own stamps and passports. Its return to Malta was celebrated by a colorful procession through the streets of Valletta, with participants dressed in black robes embroidered with the white eight-pointed cross of the Order.

GOVERNMENT

FULL DEMOCRACY CAME LATE TO MALTA. During the 20th century, the British granted various limited forms of representative government to the Maltese, but whenever these governments reached decisions that were unpalatable to the British they simply removed them. This happened several times—in 1903, 1930, 1933, and 1958.

Nevertheless, Malta has enjoyed a free press from as early as 1839, and voting by secret ballot has been the practice since 1849, when the country's first constitution, which gave the Maltese little say in political matters, was promulgated. When the country finally achieved control over its own affairs in the early 1960s, the Maltese people were more than ready to take over the reins of power.

Opposite: **Presidential guards on horseback.**

Left: **The prime minister's office in Valletta.**

THE CONSTITUTION

Malta became an independent state in 1964, following a system of parliamentary democracy based on regular elections and universal suffrage. Until 1974, when the country became a republic, Malta still recognized the British monarch, and a governor-general representing the crown resided in Valletta. Today, the head of state is the president. Although the president appoints the prime minister and the leader of the opposition, he or she does not hold political power. Executive power rests with the prime minister, who chooses a cabinet of ministers to govern the country.

Malta remains a member of the Commonwealth but is not a member of the North Atlantic Treaty Organization (NATO). Malta's foreign policy is governed by a commitment to neutrality and the constitution does not allow the country to join a military alliance or allow foreign military bases on its territory.

British and Russian ships docked at a Maltese port.

THE PARTY SYSTEM

The first political parties were formed at the end of the 19th century when the educated elite, unhappy with plans by the British to promote the English language at the expense of Italian, began to organize an opposition. The Nationalist Party developed from this pro-Italian group, while another group, supporting the promotion of English, became the Constitutional Party in the 1920s.

Today, Maltese politics is dominated by two main parties—the Nationalist Party and the Labor Party. There are 69 members in the Maltese parliament. The Labor Party was once able to command a majority of seats in the House of Representatives, even though it received a smaller number of total votes than the Nationalist Party. As a result, election rules were changed in the 1990s so that whichever party gains an absolute majority of votes will form the new government, even if this means creating additional seats in parliament. However, the Labor Party has accused the Nationalists of having engineered a built-in electoral advantage because of the way they have divided up the electoral areas.

Although many Maltese would forcefully argue against the idea, the difference between the two parties is not enormous. In the past, perhaps, the differences were meaningful ones, but in recent years the only significant divide has been the different attitudes toward joining the European Union.

The Nationalist Party is more supportive of the move, while the Labor Party has tended to focus on the terms of membership. But while the differences between the parties may seem insignificant to outsiders, this does not mean that political debate is muted. The opposite is often the case and politics remains a divisive and highly passionate affair for many Maltese.

If the United States had the same proportion of representatives as Malta, roughly one to 500 people, there would be 50,000 members of Congress!

33

SYMBOLS OF THE STATE

THE EMBLEM The emblem of Malta consists of a shield that carries a heraldic image of the national flag. At the top is a gold crown with a sally port and eight turrets (although only five are visible)—these represent the fortifications of Malta. Around the shield is a wreath of olive leaves on one side and a palm frond on the other, both symbols of peace that are traditionally associated with the country. At the bottom of the wreath is a white ribbon with the words *Repubblika ta' Malta* (Republic of Malta).

THE NATIONAL FLAG The national flag of Malta consists of two equal vertical stripes of white and red. A representation of the George Cross, awarded to Malta in 1942 in recognition of the islands' tremendous bravery in World War II, appears in the top left-hand corner of the white stripe. Tradition has it that the white and red colors were awarded to Malta by Count Roger I, the Norman ruler of Sicily, in appreciation for the hospitality shown him in 1090 when he ousted the Arabs.

There is also a maritime flag of Malta. This consists of a red field bordered in white and bearing in the center a Maltese cross in white.

THE NATIONAL ANTHEM The music for Malta's national anthem was written before the lyrics were thought of. The music was given to a well-known priest-poet, Dun Karm, in the early 1920s to write a school hymn. He used the music to write a prayer that would unite the different political opinions of the Maltese and in 1945 it became the official national anthem:

Guard her, O Lord, as ever Thou hast guarded!
This Motherland so dear whose name as bear!
Keep her in mind, whom Thou hast made so fair!

May he who rules, for wisdom be regarded!
In master mercy, strength in man increase!
Confirm us all, in unity and peace!

A STILL-POWERFUL CHURCH

The Catholic Church in Malta has a long tradition of playing a decisive role in the government of the country. For centuries before there was any democratic government the majority of people looked to their local church for guidance on nonspiritual as well as religious matters. After the British first introduced a very limited form of self-government people continued to turn to their priests for advice. At the same time, the Church was eager to ensure that its power and influence would not be eroded by support for secular politicians.

Problems arose when disagreements between the Church and the Labor Party began. In the 1950s and 1960s matters came to a head when Dom Mintoff confronted the political power and ambitions of the Church. In the 1962 election, the Church told the people of Malta, who were overwhelmingly Catholic, that it would be a sin to vote for the Labor Party and that even reading a Labor Party newspaper was against God's wishes. The opposition Nationalist Party won the 1962 election and was reelected in 1966 when the Church again sided with the Nationalist Party and warned people not to vote for Labor.

When the Labor Party formed the government in 1955, it tried to limit the power of the Church by subjecting it to taxation and by removing the immunity of the archbishop and bishops from the authority of the criminal and civil courts. Attempts to limit the power of the Church in education were less successful and serve as a reminder that the Church is still a powerful force in Maltese politics.

Eddie Fenech-Adami was prime minister from 1987 to 1996 and returned to power after a snap election in 1998.

POLITICS TODAY

In 1996 a Labor government was formed after a decade of Nationalist rule but with a majority of only one seat. This slender majority, combined with in-fighting within the Labor Party, led to a snap election in September 1998. The Nationalists won and Eddie Fenech-Adami became the prime minister. Fenech-Adami (born in 1934) succeeded to the leadership of his party in 1977 and had led the Nationalists to victory in previous elections. Malta is once again plotting a course for membership in the European Union, and although this time it looks likely to succeed, it is not a foregone conclusion because a referendum will have to held.

In the past, whenever a new government was formed, one of the first tasks of the new political leadership was to appoint party supporters to important positions in all the government departments and state-owned companies, such as the banks and the national airline. This practice was not implemented after the last two elections, perhaps a sign that Malta's politics are falling more in line with that of other European nations.

THE JUDICIARY

The term "judiciary" refers to the system whereby judges administer justice in a country. One of the central features of democratic countries is that the judiciary remains separate from the "executive," which refers to that part of the country's system of government that holds political power and that makes decisions as a result of having that power.

In Malta judges and magistrates are appointed by the president and cannot be removed from office just because a different party gains power or because the government disagrees with a judgment of the courts. There is also a special Constitutional Court that decides on matters arising from the constitution and on matters relating to human rights. Maltese law follows the principle common to American and British justice that the guilt of a person, not their innocence, has to be proven in a court.

The law courts in Valletta. The Maltese police, the *pulizija* ("PULL-IT-see-ya"), are an unarmed force. The blue uniform of its officers is another legacy of British rule.

ECONOMY

MALTA, A COUNTRY THAT POSSESSES no natural resources apart from its people and its ports, has a healthy economy that saw an average growth of 4.7% from 1992 to 1997. Inflation (the rate at which prices of goods and services increase) has averaged a low 3% a year in the 1990s, while unemployment, at less than 5% in 1997, is considerably less of a problem than in many European nations. The most important economic issue facing Malta is its planned entry into the Economic Union (EU).

THE GROSS DOMESTIC PRODUCT

The Gross Domestic Product (GDP) is the total value of goods and services produced by a country over a set period, usually a year. For Malta the GDP

Opposite: **Fishermen at Julian's Bay near Valletta.**

Left: **A farm worker sprays crops in Gozo.**

Quarry workers on the job. Most of Malta's limestone is used in the local construction industry.

averages about US$8,500 per person. One of the largest contributions to the GDP comes from manufacturing. In the past this sector was dominated by the clothing and textile industries. Today, however, the electronics industry is becoming increasingly important. The government offers various tax concessions and other financial benefits to encourage companies to set up businesses in Malta, and this is proving very successful. Another significant manufacturing activity is the ship-repair industry. This is a more traditional part of Malta's economy and originated in the days when Britain maintained dockyards to service its navy and commercial fleets. About one-quarter of Malta's working population is employed in manufacturing.

The single largest contribution to the GDP comes from tourism and other services. The growing number of visitors, now over a million a year, makes tourism a crucial part of the country's economy. The government's success in promoting Malta as an international business center has also contributed significantly to Malta's economy.

TOURISM

Tourism is a major earner of foreign currency and any sudden decline in the number of visitors would be disastrous for the economy. Over 20% of the GDP is accounted for by tourism and government policy aims to further increase this figure. Britain accounts for just under half the total number of visitors, followed by Germany and Italy. Lace-making is a traditional handicraft in Malta that has been harnessed to the tourist market. There are no factories, as this is still a home-based industry practiced entirely by women whose hand-crocheted work is now applied to far more than lace. Blouses, skirts, and shawls are painstakingly made by women in their own homes and sold directly to craft and other tourist-oriented shops.

Three times the population of Malta visit the islands each year as tourists.

A woman making lace in Gozo. Malta is renowned for its delicate lace.

Malta's docks still play a significant role in the economy. Malta's huge dry-docks can accommodate ships of 330,000 tons (300,000 metric tons) and a variety of oceangoing vessels are now built and repaired there.

THE DOCKS

The country's dock corporation is mainly owned by the government (61%), but Libya has a 30% share and Algeria 9%. The corporation employs thousands of workers to build and repair ships. The origins of this industry go back to the years of imperial rule when Britain's navy and commercial interests required a docking base in the middle of the Mediterranean. When the British pulled out of Malta in the 1970s, the economic implications for the country were grave since many people were employed on the docks. The country, however, has made good use of this asset and has developed its commercial possibilities considerably. Nevertheless, substantial government subsidies are still required.

Malta has also developed the large harbor area around Marsaxlokk, on the eastern side of the island, into an international distribution center for shipping and business. Special storage facilities are available for the blending and storing of oil products and vast warehouses have been constructed for holding shipments of all sizes.

TRADE

Malta's main exports are machinery, transportation and electronics equipment, and manufactured and semimanufactured goods. Principal imports are food, chemicals, fuels, manufactured goods, and machine parts. Germany, Italy, Britain, France, and Singapore are Malta's principal trading partners. Libya is an important source of energy and mineral fuel. In 1997 Malta's total exports were worth some US$2.8 billion, while total imports were valued at about US$3.0 billion.

The Maltese lira is the basic unit of currency.

TO JOIN OR NOT TO JOIN

Whether to join the European Union or not is the major economic issue facing Malta over the next few years. Three-quarters of the country's exports go to EU countries, and the same high percentage accounts for the origin of imports into the country. But there are also sound arguments against joining and the issue remains a controversial one. Largely due to Malta's tradition as a nonaligned state, and its willingness to trade with a variety of nations, the country enjoys healthy economic ties with non-EU states in North Africa and elsewhere. These ties would be at risk if EU membership was obtained. The shipbuilding industry, which is still an important source of employment, is partially protected by the government, which levies taxes on trading competitors.

The EU, on the other hand, is based on a fundamental commitment to free trade. Such protective levies would have to be lifted if Malta becomes a member. Perhaps even more crucial is the fact that Malta's large national debt would not be tolerated by the EU—this means the government would have to implement ways of saving money. Such cost-saving measures would not be popular with the general population, making it politically more difficult to carry through what the EU is likely to demand as the price of membership.

THE MALTESE

MALTA IS NOT A MULTIETHNIC SOCIETY and the Maltese are a remarkably homogenous people. This helps to explain the strong sense of national pride that binds the people together. However, as its long history makes clear, the country has been conquered and ruled by a series of more powerful nations, and Malta has only been an independent nation since 1964.

It is not surprising, therefore, that facial features reveal a mix of influences. Although a highly individual race, the face of a Maltese reflects a fairly unique fusion of the West (through the rule of ancient Rome and later European powers) and an Arab influence that goes back to the days of the Phoenicians.

Opposite and left: **The Maltese people have often been described by others as gregarious and friendly.**

A Maltese girl in medieval costume at Fort St. Elmo.

CHARACTERISTICS

Because the Maltese have been exposed for so long to other cultural influences, many national characteristics are the result of a blending of foreign cultures. To a lesser or greater degree, this is true of nearly all cultures, but it applies particularly to the Maltese. A good example is the very strong attachment to the Roman Catholic faith and its practices that is also found in Italy and especially Sicily, which is closer to Malta than to the Italian mainland.

An important difference, and one which goes some way to explaining what is unique about the Maltese, is Malta's internationalism. The country has been, and continues to be because of mass tourism, remarkably open to foreign influences.

Yet despite this, the people maintain their own dignity and way of life without feeling threatened or aggrieved in any way. The "no little kindness" that the Bible records as being afforded to St. Paul is an aspect of Maltese hospitality that many tourists feel is a distinguishing and highly attractive aspect of the culture. Many foreign tourists enjoy coming to the country because they feel they are treated with the same respect that the Maltese extend to their own people.

Many Maltese have a strong, almost old-fashioned, sense of dignity and manners. This is partly because Malta is not subjected to the relentless pace of modern European society. The more relaxed lifestyle allows people to interact with others in a way that seems almost stress-free.

POPULATION

The current population of Malta is 375,000, including about 28,600 on Gozo. This makes the country one of the world's more heavily populated areas. This is especially true of the main island of Malta, where about half the total population live in a small urban area around Valletta and the Grand Harbor. One reason for this comparatively large population is because the Church has been able to discourage the use of contraception and, until recently at least, families tended to be large.

About the same number of Maltese, 370,000, live overseas, mostly in Australia and Canada. The population of Malta also undergoes a massive, although temporary, surge every summer when a million tourists fly in to enjoy the hospitable climate, the beaches, and the welcoming atmosphere. About half a million summer visitors are from Britain.

The British also make up the majority of the 5,000 foreign residents who live on the islands. Many of them are senior citizens who have chosen to retire in Malta.

Every year the resident population in Malta is swelled by the one million visitors who flock to the islands to savor their attractions.

GOZITANS

About 28,600 people live on the island of Gozo, and although they are obviously Maltese, they always refer to themselves as Gozitans. This is more an expression of their sense of pride than a wish to be independent of Malta. The people of Gozo have a sense of their own identity as islanders, but there is no serious political disagreement with the Maltese government nor any wish to be treated as a separate group. There are, however, some noticeable differences in outlook between the people who live on the island of Malta and those who have lived all their lives in Gozo. Gozitans are more accustomed to a rural way of life and, up until very recently, have not benefited as much from economic progress.

A Gozitan and his donkey cart.

NICKNAMES

Nicknames, as a familiar way of identifying certain people, are common to many cultures around the world, but in Malta they were woven into the fabric of everyday life. In rural communities they still play a part in social life. According to sociologists, the relatively limited number of surnames available in Malta accounts for the common practice of identifying individuals by nicknames. One village, consisting of nearly 250 different households, was found to have less than 60 surnames, so the use of nicknames can be seen to serve a practical purpose.

What is interesting about the use of nicknames in Malta is that they can be used as a familiar term of address. This is fairly unique to Malta. In neighboring Mediterranean cultures, such as Sicily, for example, many nicknames are insults and would never be used to actually address a person. Maltese nicknames, by comparison, are mostly harmless ones. For example, a man whose hobby is catching birds with a homemade trap may be known by the name of a particular species of bird.

A FREE THINKER

Edward De Bono, one of the world's most famous psychologists, is renowned for his popular books on ways of educating the mind to think more creatively. The phrase "lateral thinking," as opposed to conventional ways of thinking that seek to categorize knowledge in an unimaginative manner, is often associated with De Bono.

He is considered by many to be a pioneer in the field of psychology and someone whose ideas have important implications for methods of teaching and learning. De Bono was born in Malta in 1933 and studied medicine there, before going to England where he also studied psychology.

Jean Parisot de la Valette, who led the Knights to their great victory over the Turks in 1565, is one of the most famous persons in Malta's long history. He joined the Order of St. John at the age of 20 and was elected Grand Master in 1557, at the age of 63. His tomb in the church of St. John in Valletta bears an inscription commemorating "the scourge of Africa and Asia and the shield of Europe."

LIFESTYLE

THE UNHURRIED PACE OF LIFE is a central characteristic of Maltese life and it is reflected in the people's lifestyle in various ways. The Maltese work hard but not to the extreme. They enjoy good conversation and exchanging news, and the many festive events bear testimony to their capacity to enjoy life outside of work. The Maltese lifestyle could very generally be described as a Mediterranean one, but there are individual inflections that are uniquely Maltese.

THE WORKING DAY

Most working Maltese tend to rise early. Farmers and other outdoor workers often start work around seven in the morning. Office workers and employees in manufacturing plants and factories usually start work an hour later or nine at the latest, and by this time shops are generally open.

Opposite: **A man and his dog greet the day.**

Left: **A woman does her laundry at a public wash-house in Gozo.**

Small bakeries and butchers open early in the morning and vendors selling fresh vegetables set up in their regular locations by erecting a small table extension from the open rear of their small vans. Many shops close for a few hours during the hottest part of the afternoon. This afternoon rest period, the *siesta* ("see-ES-ta"), is common to most Mediterranean cultures. Nevertheless, some visitors may find it strange that so many places close and then spring back to life in the late afternoon when shops remain open until about 7 p.m.

The relaxed pace of the Maltese lifestyle is typified by the absence of the modern supermarket so common in other parts of Western Europe and in North America. In Malta, people have time to shop and do not expect, or in many cases even wish, to find everything on their shopping list under one roof. Fresh meat, bread, and vegetables are still mostly bought from small vendors, who each draw customers from a recognized area.

STREET MARKETS

Virtually every town and village in Malta has a designated market area, although it may be tucked away in a side street or situated in one of the quieter corners of the town. If a visitor turned up after midday, there would be nothing to see or buy, as most of the vendors would have packed up and shoppers gone home by 11 a.m. In some of the larger towns, a street is blocked off to traffic on market day as vendors turn up in their vans and set up their trestle tables according to a strict pattern. Fresh produce such as vegetables and fish are at one end of the street reserved for their displays, while clothes and household items usually dominate the opposite end of the street or the other side of the square.

The Sunday market in Valletta always draws a big crowd.

HOMES

The people of Malta enjoy a modest and quiet lifestyle, characterized by a self-contentment that is reflected in the typical Maltese home. From the outside, there is often little to distinguish one home from another and very few people go out of their way to assert individuality or extravagant wealth. The common use of large blocks of pale-colored limestone as building material for construction helps contribute to this apparent uniformity.

MARKET DAY

Many of the items that in other parts of Europe or North America would be bought in a supermarket or specialty store are readily available on market day in Maltese towns and villages. Apart from various types of food but excluding meat and bread, market day is the occasion for buying clothing, household goods ranging from can-openers to small carpets, as well as decorative figures for display in the home.

Some items have prices marked, but the majority do not and some friendly bargaining is usual. Malta's biggest market takes place every Sunday morning outside the walls of Valletta near the main bus terminal. There is also a food market inside Valletta on weekdays. Market days in Malta also fulfill an important social role—local residents can meet their neighbors and friends in an informal setting and exchange news and gossip.

The high temperatures that characterize the long summer months have influenced the choice of building materials inside the house. Most modern homes have floors made of smooth marble or ceramic tiles because they do not retain heat.

There is a common sense of pride in keeping the interior spotlessly clean. Invariably a room is set aside as the "best room," a sitting room reserved for receiving guests. It is here that a family asserts its social identity. The best furniture is placed in this room and framed photographs of the family are hung from the walls or perhaps placed on a cabinet that contains drinks for the social occasions that bring guests into the house.

A reasonably well-to-do home usually has certain items of furniture and decoration. Crystal chandeliers, often of the highly-ornate kind, are very popular, as is handmade wooden furniture. A special chest or cabinet will be regularly polished so that it gleams as if new.

THE FARMING LIFE

The typical farm is small and family-run. Malta's rocky terrain and generally poor soil does not support large-scale farming, and there are few large commercial farms dedicated to a single crop. Many farms, especially on Gozo, which has some reasonably good agricultural land, grow a surprisingly rich variety of vegetables. Potatoes, onions, tomatoes, cabbage, lettuce, and cauliflower are grown throughout the year. Malta's warm temperatures also enable eggplant, pumpkins, figs, oranges, and lemons to be grown.

In addition, the hospitable climate allows for up to four crops of potatoes to be planted in the same year, so a small farmer can keep busy

A farmer in Marsaxlokk tends to her flock of sheep.

throughout the year. Much of the farmer's produce goes to the weekly markets in local villages and towns. Some farmers park their vans on a street corner and display baskets and cases of their produce.

On Gozo, traditional farms that have changed little in the last 50 years can still be found. A television aerial or a satellite dish may be attached to the exterior of the house, but the design of the house and the lifestyle of its inhabitants are still rooted in a rural tradition of self-sufficiency and hard work. Farm houses may be over 100 years old, and although equipped with modern household appliances, the architecture remains more Arab than European. Houses tend to be flat-roofed, small, and square, and built of honey-colored stone that merges with the natural colors of the landscape. The floors are also built with blocks of stone that are kept clean and cool by regular oiling and polishing.

Gozo produces some 60% of the agricultural produce of the Maltese archipelago. More than 3,000 Gozitans earn a living, either full-time or part-time, from agriculture.

THE GOZO LIFESTYLE

The Maltese lifestyle can generally be described as relaxed and laid-back when compared to other European countries and North America, but even Malta island seems hectic compared to its small neighboring island of Gozo. It was only recently that the first two sets of traffic lights were installed on the island and the volume of traffic is still remarkably light. The main roads are lined with white and red oleander and the absence of industry and factories give the island an atmosphere of tranquillity.

Gozo has 13 villages but 50 churches, indicating the pervasive role of religion in the islanders' lifestyle. The summer festivals are marked by fireworks and marching bands, but the religious basis to these celebrations is strongly felt by most Gozitans.

The extended family is still the norm on the island and a home shared by two or three generations is common. Rural values of thrift and conservatism are deeply rooted among Gozitans.

The University of Malta is the oldest university in the Commonwealth outside of Britain. The university's history dates back to 1592, when the Jesuits founded the college, which became renowned for its scholarship throughout the Mediterranean. In 1768 it became a university.

EDUCATION

School attendance is compulsory from the ages of 5 to 16 and is free in government schools and institutions, from kindergarten to university. Kindergarten classes cater to 3- and 4-year-olds. Children attend elementary school until the age of 11, before going on to secondary education. Some students go to a trade school or craft center after three years of secondary education, where they pursue less academic and more practical subjects. Others take examinations at the age of 16.

Every year, well over half the number of students reaching the age of 16 continue their education. A variety of post-secondary courses are available to students, ranging from academic programs designed as pre-university courses to vocational programs in such areas as tourism, agriculture, healthcare, and technical education. The University of Malta, which has over 6,000 Maltese students at any one time, also attracts several hundred students from neighboring Mediterranean and Middle Eastern countries.

The Church still plays an important role in education and runs its own schools alongside state schools. These religious schools are subsidized by the government and are not allowed to charge student fees.

POLITICS

Politics is woven into the fabric of Maltese life in a way that is quite different than in the United States. Although the situation is changing, especially among the younger generation of Maltese, there is still much truth to the notion that a Maltese is born into a political party. Family loyalties are often closely tied to one of the two main parties, and this operates at a very basic level. It is not unknown for a family to prefer to shop at a particular place, or even more strongly wish to avoid a particular shop, because of the proprietor's political beliefs.

BUS TRAVEL

Buses in Malta, beside being a means of transportation, are very much a part of the Maltese lifestyle. Although car ownership is very high, public transportation still plays an important role in many people's lives. This is especially true of older citizens and young people who do not have their own cars.

Since a seven-mile (11-km) stretch of railway was closed in 1931, the bus network has been the sole means of public transportation and has spread to encompass nearly every corner of the island. The hub of the bus network, and the place from which nearly all the island's buses operate, is a large square and roundabout immediately outside the walls of Valletta.

The bus terminal in Valletta.

No village on the island of Malta is more than an hour's journey by bus to the capital.

From about 6 a.m. until around 11 p.m., this area bustles with activity as a constant stream of pale green and chrome buses move in and out. Although Malta has some modern air-conditioned vehicles, decades-old buses are more common. Lending individuality to the buses is the way their exteriors are decorated with various stickers and metal emblems. It is not uncommon to find a nickname or pet name for the bus emblazoned across the hood.

THE KAROZZIN

A more traditional form of transportation, dating back to the mid-19th century, is the horse-drawn carriage known as *karozzin* ("ca-rotts-SEEN"). They hold up to four passengers on high seats, with a canopy to provide shade. They are still used by some Maltese, especially on Gozo, for short trips, such as a social visit to friends on a Sunday.

VEHICLE WORSHIP

There is about one car for every two adults in Malta and very few families do not own a vehicle. But as not everyone can afford a new car, few cars are scrapped. Most Maltese, at one time or another, deal with the second-hand car market, and older cars that would rapidly lose their value in other parts of Europe keep their value for a lot longer. Small auto repair businesses are common, and many Maltese take great pride in keeping a car in running condition that is no longer manufactured.

It is this tradition of looking after old cars that helps explain the regard that many people have toward vehicles. Owners like to decorate their cars with stickers and emblems, and trucks and public buses get special treatment. The driver's area of a public bus may even be transformed into a mini-shrine with the help of small plastic statues, religious pictures and icons, and dried flowers in glass vases.

Cars more than 20 years old are commonplace on Malta's roads.

RELIGION

MALTA IS STRONGLY AND PREDOMINANTLY Roman Catholic, yet its Catholicism has qualities unlike those of other Catholic countries. This is evident in the multitude of festivals that take place every year, for although they nearly all have a religious origin, they are regarded by many Maltese as festive, social events.

Like many other European countries, Malta has changed with the times. The Roman Catholic Church no longer wields the enormous power it once had over people's daily lives. Besides Catholicism, there are several other religious groups in Malta, including Anglicans, Methodists, Greek Orthodox, Jews, Muslims, and some small evangelical groups. Under the country's constitution, Roman Catholicism is the state religion and must be taught in state schools.

Opposite: **A statue of Madonna in Mdina.**

Left: **A group of girls at their first communion.**

CHRISTIANITY

According to legend, Christianity came to Malta with one of Christ's disciples, St. Paul, who was shipwrecked on the island. At the time, Malta was occupied by the Romans and St. Paul was brought to the capital and allowed to preach Christianity. The Roman governor, Publius, and his family were converted and he ordered that Christianity become the religion of the country. In this way, Malta became one of the first countries in the world to adopt Christianity.

The period of Arab domination interrupted Christian rule, but it was resumed with the arrival of the Normans who reestablished the religion on an official basis. In 1530 the Knights of the Order of St. John arrived on the island, giving a new impetus to the hold of the religion over the people. After a very short period of anticlerical French rule under Napoleon, the Church reestablished its power during the 19th and 20th centuries.

Under British rule, the missionary activities of other churches were restricted, and in 1922 the Roman Catholic religion was recognized in law as the religion of the country. A section of the Malta Criminal Code was passed making it a criminal offense to criticize the Catholic religion in public. It is this long, uninterrupted, and unchallenged period of Catholic influence that is still felt today in Malta.

As late as the 1950s, the Church dominated social life and determined the educational and social activities of the young in ways that are no longer acceptable in Western countries. The Church ran its own schools, paid no

The shipwreck of St. Paul off the coast of Malta. The Maltese believe this event led to the introduction of Christianity on the island.

taxes, and owned large tracts of land and property on the islands. Priests could not be prosecuted under Maltese law. The disputes of the 1950s and 1960s with the Labor Party postponed the inevitable decline of Church power but could not prevent it. Today, religion in Malta is no longer a matter of social pressure but one of choice.

The islands of Malta form an archdiocese, with an archbishop based in Valletta and two cathedrals. Gozo has its own bishop. The islands have more than 350 churches, many of them medieval in origin, and there are about 900 priests. Fifty-six homes for Christian brothers and 103 convents are also found on the islands.

HOW TO UPSET EVERYONE IN EIGHT DAYS

Napoleon brought 700 years of Christian rule in Malta to an abrupt end when in 1798 the French drove the Knights from the islands. Napoleon himself only remained in Malta for eight days, but in that time he tried to make too many changes too quickly and stirred up popular discontent as a result.

Some of the changes he instituted were well-received, such as establishing a council of Maltese to administer the islands and creating government schools, but his attacks on the power of the Church misfired. He set up civil marriages so that people could wed outside of a church, limited the power of Malta's bishop to purely church affairs, and abolished the practice in which members of the clergy could charge fees for their services. To make matters worse, the French did not have enough money to ensure the changes were made smoothly, so they attempted to auction off the property of a church in Mdina. Led by influential Christians, the people rose in rebellion and the main French force had to take refuge in Valletta.

According to tradition, there are no poisonous snakes in Malta because St. Paul removed all their venom after being bitten by one soon after he arrived.

ROMAN CATHOLICISM

Roman Catholicism emphasizes the role of the Virgin Mary. Small grottoes dedicated to the mother of Christ are maintained throughout the island. Another way in which the Roman Catholic Church differs from other forms of Christianity is in the role of the head of the Church, the Pope. His decisions are considered infallible, which means that the various encyclicals that are issued by the Vatican must be followed by all Catholics. On a tiny island like Malta, which has had a serious problem with overpopulation for some time, the Church's restriction on birth control has caused much soul-searching. This issue was part of the battle that took place between the Church and the Labor Party in the 1950s and 1960s.

SAINT PAUL

Originally a Jew from Asia Minor, St. Paul was born in A.D. 6 and trained as a rabbi. In his early years he actively persecuted Christians, believing them to be a breakaway Jewish sect, but on a journey to Damascus one day he had a vision of Christ telling him to become a missionary for Christianity. His life thereafter was a series of missionary journeys across Greece and as far as Malta, where he was shipwrecked en route to Rome.

The Church of St. Paul in Rabat is said to be the first parish church on the islands. Near it is a grotto where the saint is believed to have spent most of his time while on Malta. The walls of the grotto are believed to have miraculous curative properties. Beneath the church are catacombs built into the soft limestone rock where tables have been carved into the rock for people to celebrate Christ's last supper. On his return from Malta, St. Paul was arrested after riots by Jewish groups against his preaching and was executed in Rome in A.D. 62.

PRACTICE AND SUPERSTITIONS

Most Maltese have a personal saint to whom they appeal in times of need. Many churches hold collections of votive paintings dedicated to a particular saint after an intercession or a cure, as well as other items dedicated to the saint, such as crutches no longer needed after a miracle cure. Shrines dot the island—in small grottoes, in offices and shops, and even in buses. As in many other Catholic countries people make the sign of the cross as they pass a church and stand still at the midday and evening angelus when the church bells are rung.

For most people in Malta, there is a point where religious belief mixes with superstition. For example, the design of some baroque churches on the island is part superstition and part practicality. These churches have two towers and one tower always contains a clock, which in the olden days was the only clock in the whole village. To keep the symmetry of the church front, another clock was put on the other tower. Since a real clock was too expensive and unnecessary, a clock face was often painted on the tower. The time on the painted clock face always shows a few minutes before midnight, the witching hour. At midnight the devil is said to roam, looking for souls. Seeing the hands of the clock at 11:55 p.m. confuses the devil and prevents him from carrying out his evil work.

A shrine in Rabat—one of many found in Malta.

There are many other signs of superstition in Malta. Women wear coral necklaces to ward off evil, while many rural houses have a pair of bull's horns tied high up on a corner of the house. A niche around the house may also hold a figure of a saint. Another example of superstition on the islands are the *luzzijiet* ("LUT-tsie-yiet"), the fishing boats that are always named after a saint and have eyes painted on the stern to keep the boats watchful. The painted eyes, known as the eyes of Osiris, after an ancient Egyptian god, are regarded by the superstitious as a means of warding off evil, but their use today is more as a traditional symbol of good luck.

NON GODE IMMUNITA ECCLESIASTICA

This is an ancient Latin phrase that can be translated as "Do not hold this church to be free from the law." It is often seen by the main door of small churches around the island. The phrase dates back to the period before the 19th century when the church had sole jurisdiction over all matters within its property, much like modern-day embassies where the laws of the host country do not apply.

Criminals on the run could seek sanctuary in a church. In order to prevent churches from filling up with criminals, the church authorities put up these signs giving up church jurisdiction wherever the signs were posted. Churches without the Latin inscription could, however, still be used for sanctuary. In 1828 the British governor proclaimed an end to the sanctuary law.

THE CHRISTIAN CALENDAR

In Malta the major Christian festivals are celebrated in traditional style. A Maltese tradition at Christmas is to give children shallow saucers of water in which are sown wheat seeds or other seeds. The seeds are kept in the dark until they sprout. They are then placed by the family's nativity scene, by the crib of the baby Jesus. This tradition may be a remnant of an earlier religion in which the harvest was significant.

Easter is traditionally celebrated with a procession on Good Friday. Penitents make the journey in as uncomfortable a way as they can. Young men are often hooded and wear white robes with heavy chains on their ankles. The belief is that the farther they can walk in such discomfort the more of their sins will be forgiven.

Every village has its own patron saint, and the feast day of that saint is always celebrated on the nearest weekend. Where once this was a religious event, the majority of people today see it as a secular occasion.

Firework displays have become an important part of festivities to celebrate the patron saints.

CELEBRATING THE PATRON SAINT

Malta's traditional festivals are primarily social occasions today, but they still retain a religious significance based on the worship of a patron saint of a village or town. The pealing of church bells may be drowned out by the sound of exploding fireworks, but for devout Catholics a visit to their church is the most important part of these festivities. Much effort and care goes into decorating the church inside and outside, and the climax of the event is still the procession where a life-size statue of the patron saint is paraded through the streets.

Three days of prayer precede the festival. Every evening, singing takes place in the church, followed by Mass and a special service known as the benediction. Each village has its own hymn to its patron saint in a popular melody and an anthem set to operatic music. These evening services end with members of the congregation kissing the saint's relic, which is enshrined in an ornately-decorated gold case called the monstrance.

On the eve of the feast day, another special service takes place in the church. When Mass is over, a hymn of praise, known as the *Te Deum* ("tay

NICCEC

Around the islands at the numerous shrines to the saints are objects known as *niccec* ("nee-chech"), padlocked boxes embedded in the shrine. These are contributions boxes where those in search of intercession from the saint can drop in some money, which goes to the local church or a charity.

DAY-um"), from the first words of the Latin hymn, is sung. The life-sized statue of the saint rests overnight in the center of the nave and bouquets of flowers are arranged around it as an act of homage. In the evening the holy relic is solemnly carried from a side chapel to the main altar.

On the evening of the feast day itself, the statue of the saint is carried shoulder-high out of the church and through the streets, while the relic of the saint is solemnly carried by a church dignitary. Monks and priests, dressed in their finest vestments, join the procession alongside lay members of devotional associations. These members wear their own colorful robes and walk behind their own huge banner displaying an emblem of their group.

A procession honoring a patron saint attracts a huge crowd of believers and spectators.

SOME OTHER SAINTS

Each tiny village in Malta has its own saint, as does each profession. Some of the saints have particularly gruesome stories of martyrdom. St. Agatha, whose chapel is in Mdina, is the patron saint of Malta. She fled to Malta from Italy in A.D. 249, after refusing to marry the governor of Catania at the wish of Emperor Decius. In Malta she was said to have spent her time in catacombs under the city, teaching and praying. When she left Malta and returned to Catania in 251, she was imprisoned and tortured before being burned to death.

St. Luke is another famous person to have spent time on the island. He accompanied Paul on his journeys. A physician, he is the patron saint of doctors, students, butchers, and artists. St. Publius converted Malta to Christianity. He was made bishop of Malta and then Athens. Later martyred, he became a saint.

Decorations pay homage to one of Malta's many saints, St. Catherine.

ANCIENT RELIGIONS

The temples at Ggantija are believed to be the oldest freestanding monuments in the world, predating the pyramids. The remains of the temples suggest an earth-worshipping civilization with complex religious ceremonies. Altars show evidence of animal sacrifice with libations of blood and milk. Priestesses could have hidden behind curtains and in hidden chambers in the rock, issuing predictions, and people may have come to the temples to ask the oracles for advice. Burials made around the same time were complex, suggesting also the earth-mother worship indicated by the temples.

Around 3000 B.C. the community built the Hypogeum, a series of underground burial chambers, at Paola. It was discovered by chance and contained fragments of bone and pottery. The walls were decorated with patterns and symbols and an oracle chamber was cut into the wall. It would have echoed the priest's voice and made it seem more supernatural. At Tarxien, a statue of the earth goddess has been discovered.

The altars at the Hagar Qim temple offer a glimpse of a vanished religion.

73

LANGUAGE

MALTA'S OFFICIAL LANGUAGES are Maltese and English. There are few people in Malta who cannot speak some English, but the Maltese language is alive and well and it is not an endangered language. Italian is also spoken, or at least understood, by many Maltese. Few citizens are monolingual. Maltese can, however, be difficult to master because of its complex pronunciation rules.

MALTESE

The Maltese language reveals the mixed history of the country. There is no evidence of influence by the Phoenician or Roman cultures, but the arrival of the Arabs in the ninth century was to have a profound effect on the language.

Opposite and left: **A large section of the Maltese population is bilingual or even trilingual. Besides Maltese and English, Italian is also understood by many people.**

The first Maltese dictionaries were compiled in the 17th century, although the earliest prose writing in Maltese that has survived is a collection of religious sermons from 1739. The language of the sermons betrays a strong Italian influence in its choice of vocabulary, which is not surprising given that the Church in Malta at that time was largely made up of Sicilians. It was only in 1934 that Maltese became the official language of the law courts, which until then had used Italian.

Here are some basic everyday expressions that you might like to try using. The first two words show a French influence and are pronounced very much like their French equivalents, while the word for "thank you" reveals the influence of Italian:

Bongu ("BON-joo")	Good morning
Bonswa ("BON-swah")	Good evening
Sahha ("sah-har")	Goodbye
Jekk joghgbok ("ye-hek YOJ-bok")	Please
Grazzi ("GRAHT-see")	Thank you
Iva ("EE-vah")	Yes
Le ("leh")	No

ARAB INFLUENCE

At a very basic structural level, Maltese can be regarded as an Arabic dialect. In terms of families of languages Maltese belongs to the Semitic group, the word Semitic being used to describe a set of languages that includes Arabic and Hebrew. That Maltese remains a Semitic language is quite remarkable considering that nearly 1,000 years have passed since the Arabs lost control of Malta to the Normans. When the Arabs first arrived, there was, of course, a language already being used by the native population, but this was effectively replaced by the language of the

conquerors. Around 10,000 Maltese words are of Semitic origin, but this is not a particularly large percentage of the total vocabulary. There are more words of non-Semitic origin in the Maltese language, but interestingly many of the basic words that belong to the ordinary, everyday world of living are Arabic in origin. This reflects how Arab influence impacted the lives of ordinary people.

That some Maltese words used to describe Christian ideas are also Arabic in origin suggest that the early Christians who came to Malta continued to use the Arabic language. Curiously, the Maltese word for "father," *missier* ("MISS-ir"), is a Romance word, while *omm* ("OMM"), the word for "mother," is Arabic. This might be because the Normans, who first introduced Romance words to Malta, would have intermarried with native, Arabic-speaking women. In this way the two cultures kept their hold on the common language that eventually evolved.

Although there are thousands of words of Italian and Sicilian origin in the Maltese language today, the basic structure of the language remains Arabic.

ROMANCE INFLUENCE

Romance languages—the main ones being Italian, French, and Spanish—are languages that developed from the spoken form of Latin used in the Roman Empire. It was the Normans who first brought a new, non-Arabic language to Malta, but while they introduced a large stock of new words from Romance vocabulary, they did not change the fundamental structure of the language, which remained Semitic.

The Norman lords who settled in Malta did not maintain the same degree of contact with the native population as the Arabs. The Maltese learned many new words, but they did not acquire a grammar that could replace the Arabic structure of the language they spoke. The input of Romance words into the Maltese vocabulary continued under the rule of the Spanish kingdoms and the Order of St. John.

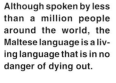

Although spoken by less than a million people around the world, the Maltese language is a living language that is in no danger of dying out.

The men who made up the Order of St. John came from the aristocratic families of Europe, and their linguistic influence was felt in Malta over a period of 250 years. Like the Normans, they did not have much contact with the peasants of the islands. So although new words were constantly being added, the structure of the language spoken by ordinary people remained largely unchanged. The earliest examples of Maltese literature date back to the 17th century.

SOME TRADITIONAL PROVERBS

The word of a Maltese is more reliable than the oath of a king.

A sleeping man catches no fish.

If you cut off the tail of a pig it will always remain a pig.

An agreement between two people is reached in two days; an agreement between three requires two months.

Expect the worst, so that the good may not be lacking.

Money breeds money and worms breed worms.

Mountain does not meet mountain, but a face meets another face.

Enjoy yourself, for there is nothing in the world we can call our own.

There is no rose without thorns.

THE ITALIAN CONNECTION

As we learned earlier, the Maltese constitution was suspended by the British in the early 1930s, mainly as the result of a controversial attempt to promote Italian as the official language. The British claimed that only about 15% of the population spoke Italian. Italy's political leader, Benito Mussolini, on the other hand, claimed that the Maltese language was a dialect of Italian and that the Maltese people were Italian by race. There was, however, no linguistic basis to this claim and the real nature of Mussolini's interest in Malta became clear when World War II broke out and Italian planes bombed the island.

ENGLISH IN MALTA

English was first introduced to Malta in the early 19th century when the British, then at war with France, took over the islands after the French garrison surrendered. At that time the ruling class in Malta, including government officials and the Church, mostly spoke Italian and little

BORROWED WORDS

FROM THE ROMANCE LANGUAGES A large part of the Maltese vocabulary is derived from words of Romance origin, especially Sicilian and Italian words. These include the majority of words associated with religious life; words for the months of the year; words used in the house such as "bedroom," "dining room," and kitchen objects; and most words relating to the ship, the army, forms of entertainment, and the different trades and professions.

FROM THE ARABIC WORLD The names for certain directions of the wind; the bastions of the city walls; words such as "roof" and "floor;" basic foods, such as *bajd* ("BITE," eggs); most names of fishes, fruits, trees, plants, and seeds; and basic verbs related to education, such as *qara* ("RA," to read), *kiteb* ("kee-TEP," to write), *ghadd* ("ADD," to count), and *tghallem* ("tull-LEMM," to learn).

changed for a long time after the arrival of the British. English made little headway in Malta in the 19th century because the British exercised political power but did not mix on a daily basis with ordinary people. In this way they were not very different from the Normans or the Knights of St. John.

It was only in the 20th century that English began to play an increasingly important role in the lives of the Maltese people. The replacement of Italian with English in the education system starting in the 1930s was pivotal because this affected ordinary young people and not just the educated elite. In the 1960s Malta developed as a popular holiday destination for British tourists. An important reason for this, apart from the appealing climate of a Mediterranean island, was the perception that Malta was

English-speaking visitors to Malta have little difficulty communicating with the Maltese because of the widespread use of English on the islands.

friendly towards the British. The long history of imperial rule had accustomed the Maltese to the habits of the British, and English was not an unfamiliar language. As tourism became increasingly important to the Maltese economy, and as English established itself as the world's international language, the Maltese became more and more willing to learn and use English.

Malta enters the 21st century as a bilingual society, where English and Maltese are used fluently as the means of communication, both officially and informally.

A street sign in Maltese and English in Mdina.

THE POLITICS OF LANGUAGE

Although English is now widely spoken in Malta, the first attempts to introduce the language into the education system created much resentment among the Maltese upper class. In 1880 a British report recommended that English instead of Italian should be taught in the country's elementary schools and that only English should be used in the university. This was not well received by the country's non-British elite. This small class of educated people, supported by priests, campaigned against the idea. It was feared then that the spread of English, at the expense of Italian, would weaken the power of the Church and encourage Protestantism.

It was this controversy that led to the rise of the first Maltese political groups. The campaign against the promotion of English was successful enough to delay the proposed changes for many years. For a long time, both English and Italian were offered as the language of instruction in elementary schools. Parents opted for one or the other. In the 1930s the teaching of Italian was abolished by the British. Soon after, the Maltese government was suspended after it attempted to reintroduce Italian. The issue only came to an end with the outbreak of World War II, which brought Italy into conflict with Malta.

THE MEDIA

There are daily and weekly newspapers in English and in Maltese. British daily newspapers arrive on the evening of their day of publication, and American newspapers such as *The International Herald Tribune* are also available. Malta has one public television channel, which broadcasts mostly in Maltese but includes some news and other programs in English, and numerous radio channels. Tall television antennas and satellite dishes are a common sight because of the popularity of Italian television stations, which broadcast extensive coverage of Italian soccer games and also transmit programs that would not generally be shown on the more conservative and Church-influenced state television station.

Many people in Valletta have installed tall television antennas to receive transmissions from Italy to the north.

ARTS

SOME OF THE FINEST ART that Malta has produced is prehistoric, expressed in stone and found in the great megalithic temples that were built before the pyramids of Egypt. They represent some of the world's earliest surviving examples of art. Well over 4,000 years separate this era from the next remarkable expression of artistry in Malta when the Knights of St. John arrived in the 16th century and a second great period of building took place.

MEGALITHIC ART

The word megalithic, which is derived from the ancient Greek words for "large" and "stone," is especially apt in describing Malta's temples because some of their stones weigh over 22 tons (20 metric tons). One megalith measures 23 by 10 feet (7 by 3 m).

Very little is known about the Neolithic societies that built Malta's temples, and even less is known about why the societies suddenly collapsed sometime around 2500 B.C. As early expressions of an artistic impulse, however, their temples surpass anything that has been found in Malta from the Bronze Age, which lasted for over 1,500 years.

Opposite: **The pavement floor in St. John's Co-cathedral in Valletta is made up of marble tombstones of the Knights of St. John.**

Left: **Sculptures by Antonio Sciortino, one of Malta's most famous artists.**

85

GGANTIJA The two temples at Ggantija in Gozo, which date from around 3500 B.C., are believed to be the oldest freestanding monuments in the world. They were built as places to worship a fertility goddess, and it has been suggested that the structures were shaped to represent the head and breasts of the goddess. In the doorway of the larger temple, the holes for the hinges that held a giant set of doors can still be seen. A forecourt area stands in front of this doorway, dividing the congregation from the priests, who may have conducted their ceremonies inside.

Excavations in the early 19th century unearthed various pottery and statuettes, including a rare relief carving of a snake. These are now on display in museums in Valletta and Victoria. Legend has it that this temple

The Ggantija temples. Legend credits the construction of the temples to Sansuna, a female giant. Able to carry huge stones on her head from a local quarry, Sansuna's strength was attributed to her vegetarian diet.

was built by a female giant, which ties in with evidence of ritual worship of female fertility figures.

TARXIEN TEMPLES There are three temples at Tarxien. One of them, known as the South Temple, has a central paved square surrounded by carved stone benches. This area may have been the site for ritual fires, as the burned remains of animal bones have been excavated. A similar design characterizes the earliest of the three temples, the Central Temple, which dates from about 2400 B.C.

In one of the side rooms of this temple, there is a huge bowl that was carved from a single piece of stone. The art of this Stone Age society is revealed in various relief carvings of spirals and animals—cattle, pigs, goats, and bulls—that decorate some of the walls. At both Tarxien and other temple sites the most intriguing finds are various headless figures, known as the "fat" deities because of their obese appearance.

HAGAR QIM AND MNAJDRA TEMPLE Hagar Qim is a fan-like series of oval rooms that archeologists believe were not conceived as a single project but were added on at different times. As at Ggantija, holes have been found around the entrance where the hinges of doors once fit, again suggesting a clear division between priests and ordinary participants at temple ceremonies. Both Hagar Qim and Mnajdra, situated nearby in a more sheltered position, reveal evidence of early man's artistic endeavors—patterns of pitted and spiral designs cut into stone.

A "fat" deity at Tarxien. The figures are thought to be fertility symbols, and one such deity found at the South Temple in Tarxien is estimated to have stood more than eight feet (2.5 m) high.

THE HYPOGEUM A hypogeum is an underground chamber. When several Maltese house builders accidentally broke through the roof of one in 1902, they tried to keep it a secret because they knew the authorities would delay the construction of the house they were working on. It was a few years before the secret was revealed. Then when the site was excavated it was found to consist of three levels of catacombs.

One was a naturally-occurring structure, while the other two had been carved out of the soft limestone. They were used as burial chambers, but their greatest significance is as monumental works of art. They have survived for five millennia, as have the spiral and hexagonal designs that decorated the walls and pillars. However, they were closed to the public for many years after the discovery that the carbon dioxide breathed out by thousands of visitors every week was beginning to unsettle the delicate climatic balance of the underground environment.

The bones of about 7,000 people have been found in the Hypogeum, together with various artifacts. The Hypogeum has stood the test of time—it was used as an air-raid shelter in World War II, some 5,000 years after its construction, before mass tourism began to threaten its structural integrity.

ART OF THE KNIGHTS

The great art of Malta associated with the Knights of St. John was not the creative work of individual members of the Order. What was important was the wealth and power of the Knights, for they represented the cream of European aristocracy and used their great wealth to commission the best architects and artists to work for them. Their legacy can be found today in the unique design and architecture of Valletta, the stately *palazzos* ("PAL-at-zios," Italian mansions) they commissioned, the auberges ("ou-BERGES") they lived in, and most magnificently of all, their baroque cathedrals and other churches.

The fortified city of Valletta is perhaps the most enduring legacy of the Knights of St. John.

Work started on the construction of Valletta soon after the end of the Great Siege in 1565. Several important architects, mostly Italian, were involved, but the initial design was the work of Francesco Laparelli da Cortona (1521–70). It was he who proposed the building of a completely new city. Laparelli devised a grid system based on eight main streets running from the northwest to the southeast, and intersected by 10 other streets that were laid out perpendicularly to the main streets. The open sea protected one end of Valletta, while a huge ditch was built outside the main entrance at the other, inland, end and massive fortifications were built to defend it. These deep walls still stand today, despite heavy bombing in the area during World War II.

Laparelli died of the plague before the work was completed and his Maltese assistant, Gerolamo Cassar (1520–86), took over. Cassar was to became responsible for many of the important buildings erected by the Order, including St. John's Co-cathedral.

ST. JOHN'S CO-CATHEDRAL

The rather austere exterior of this church, completed in 1578, gives little indication of the incredible wealth of art that decorates the interior. The floor of the nave is composed of some 400 tombs of noted Knights; many of the tombs are highly individual in their design. Highly-ornate side chapels branch off from the central nave, each one dedicated to one of the European nations that the Knights came from. The Chapel of Germany has a beautiful white marble altar, while the Chapel of Italy used to contain a famous painting by Caravaggio, *St. Jerome*, which was stolen in 1984 but recovered a few years later. It is now in the secure church museum, next to another Caravaggio painting, *The Beheading of St. John the Baptist*. The Chapel of Aragon is one of the most artistic areas in the cathedral and contains a number of paintings by Mattia Preti, as well as very ornate memorial stones.

The bleak facade of St. John's Co-cathedral. Inside, the barrel-vaulted ceiling of the nave is covered in a series of 18 episodes in the life of St. John the Baptist, painted in oils by Mattia Preti.

ST. PAUL'S CATHEDRAL

Building work started on this magnificent church, a minor masterpiece of European church architecture, in 1697 and was completed five years later. The exterior is made up of three bays, each with its own door and divided by pillars. There are two bell towers. The interior is a tribute to Maltese baroque art. The 164-foot (50-m) long nave is paved with marble tombstones of notable members of society of the time, and while they are all largely forgotten today, their splendid memorial stones remain as testimony to the artisans who created them. Similar tombs are found in the side chapels.

ART GALORE

The single most important artist commissioned by the Knights was Caravaggio (1571–1610), one of the greatest Italian artists, who arrived in Malta in 1607. He was glad to leave Italy, where he was wanted for murder, and later became a Knight in Malta. After completing several paintings he became involved in a fight and was expelled from the Order. He returned to Italy, where while waiting for a pardon from the Pope, he died from malaria at the age of 38. He is noted for using ordinary working people as models for his religious paintings. St. John's Co-cathedral also contains a set of highly-artistic Flemish tapestries, which were modeled on drawings by the famous Flemish artist, Rubens.

Other fine works of art include sculptures by the Maltese Antonio Sciortino and paintings by the Venetian Domenico Tintoretto, a relative of the famous Tintoretto, and by Antoine de Favray, the French artist.

There are also a number of valuable individual works of art inside the church, including frescoes and paintings, a 15th-century marble font, and a carved door to the sacristy made of solid Irish oak. This door is part of an older church that was destroyed in an earthquake in 1693.

THE AUBERGES

The Knights who first arrived in Malta were divided into groups according to their nationalities, and each group built their own "inn of residence." Auberge is a French word meaning "inn," and the various homes of the Knights came to be known by this name. Nine auberges were built, seven of which were designed by Gerolamo Cassar between 1571 and 1575, though only four still stand today.

One of the most artistic, which was home to Knights from parts of Spain and Portugal, is the Auberge of Castile. It has three rows of windows, with scroll and shell ornamentation, and a highly-ornate doorway flanked by cannons and decorated with a bust of a Grand Master amid an array of banners and triumphal insignia. Although bombed and damaged during World War II, it has been carefully restored and is now the office of the prime minister.

The Auberge of Italy is another fine example of the artistic architecture that the Knights were able to commission. The imposing facade contains a bust of another Grand Master and his escutcheon (a shield or emblem bearing a coat of arms).

Above: **The Gobelin Tapestries in the Grand Master's Palace were based on a set of paintings by two artists who had traveled to South America and Africa in the 17th century.**

Right: **The entrance to the Grand Master's Palace.**

THE GRAND MASTER'S PALACE

Some of the more artistic buildings in Malta are Italian-style *palazzos*. They were commissioned by the Order and one of them, the Palazzo di Citta, built as a public records office in 1720, is still used for that purpose today. But for artistic achievement, few can compare with the Grand Master's Palace in Valletta. It was built in 1569 as a prestigious house for a Grand Master's nephew and was extended two years later by Gerolamo Cassar. It now occupies an entire block in the capital and houses Malta's House of Representatives.

Many of the rooms are decorated with friezes portraying events from the history of the Order and impressive portraits of various Grand Masters through the centuries. One painting is by Mateo Perez d'Aleccio, a pupil of Michelangelo. There is also an armory with extensive examples of armor and weaponry.

Perhaps the most important work of art, however, is a set of tapestries that adorn the walls of one room. The tapestries consist of 10 large panels depicting colorful animals and birds and are known as the Gobelin Tapestries after a famous factory in Paris where they were made after being commissioned by a Grand Master.

Modern-day pottery in Malta.

THE MANOEL THEATER

This beautiful, baroque theater was named after the Grand Master of the time, a Portuguese called Antonio Manoel de Vilhena. The theater is the third oldest in the world. It is still in use, and as Malta's national theater it hosts the more important plays and concerts. The Manoel Theater was built between 1722 and 1736, a time when the Knights were experiencing one of their more peaceful periods and were eager to enjoy the social activities and forms of entertainment that a theater could facilitate.

Although an inscription over the door proclaims that it was built for "the honest recreation of the people," it was reserved for the ruling class of Knights and ordinary Maltese would not have visited the place. The theater fell into disuse in the 1860s and was later used as a hostel for the poor and then a movie theater, but was restored in the 1960s. Today, its interior is stunning. The stage area is small and the stalls seat less than 300 people, but rising above them are three tiers of baroque boxes in gold and green and decorated with frescoes. Above the boxes is a gallery area, where one can even reach out and touch the gilded ceiling, which gives some indication of the intimacy of the theater.

CONTEMPORARY ART

The works of contemporary Maltese artists include paintings, prints, sculpture, jewelry, and couture. One well-known artist in Malta is Norbert Attard, whose early work includes prints of abstract geometric shapes against a spray-brushed background and who has now moved on to installation art. Joe Xuereb is a sculptor from Gozo, while Joseph Bellia is a landscape painter from the island of Malta. One of the most famous Maltese artists—and one with an international reputation—is Alfred Chircop. Sue and Anna Nightingale, mother and daughter, form a painting duo from Gozo and their work embraces both pictorial subjects and abstract themes.

ORAL POETRY

There is still a tradition of reciting poetry in Malta, and this remains a popular form of entertainment. Known as *ghana* ("ANN-aa"), the term covers a variety of poems that are sung to the musical accompaniment of guitars. Sometimes they are performed by two singers who recite their verses as if they were competing against each other. Another version takes the form of a long and complicated narrative based on the exploits of legendary figures or even contemporary events. A typical poem is a rhyming four-line verse, with each line usually having eight syllables.

This traditional art form has been given a new lease on life by young folk singers and musicians who use modern technology to record these traditional poems.

The making of lace with intricate patterns is another contemporary art form, but one which has an ancient lineage in Malta. Lace is made by women on both islands, particularly in Gozo, where women sit on their doorsteps skillfully plying the bobbins to produce their ware.

LITERATURE AND PATRIOTISM

Malta's literary tradition only started in the 19th century. Writers who have emerged include Dun Karm, the most notable Maltese poet, A. Cremona and G. Aquilina. Three moments in Maltese history recur as popular themes in Maltese literature and all three record the overcoming of an external threat—the defeat of Turkish invaders, the expulsion of Napoleon's troops in 1800, and the islands' heroic stand against aerial bombardment in World War II. The frequency with which these events are referred to suggests the importance of these moments in shaping and giving expression to Maltese national pride.

LEISURE

MALTA IS NOT A WORKAHOLIC SOCIETY and leisure time is not some precious commodity that has to be snatched from the timetable of a busy day. Leisure takes its natural place alongside the world of work and they complement, rather than compete with, each other. This is especially apparent in the refreshing practice of taking a casual stroll with a partner or a friend when the heat of the afternoon sun has subsided.

STROLLING IN THE STREET

This traditional feature of the Maltese lifestyle, that of dressing up in stylish clothes—but never overdressing—and going out for a social walk, helps define the difference between a Mediterranean culture as found in countries such as Malta and the more work-oriented, faster-paced lifestyle of northern Europe.

Opposite: **The terrace at the Upper Barrakka Gardens in Valletta offers a magnificent vantage point over the Grand Harbor.**

Left: **The beaches at Mellieha Bay are popular with the Maltese and tourists alike.**

Strolling along the waterfront is an enjoyable leisure activity for many Maltese.

Older people tend to walk in pairs, with their partner, relative, or friend, while younger people usually move in small groups. The activity provides an opportunity for informal conversation and a possible encounter with friends or neighbors who are also out walking. In towns, certain streets and routes, often the promenade that follows the course of the shoreline, are popular.

The early evening stroll is an endearing habit of the Maltese, not least because it suggests a relaxed state of mind that can enjoy a simple social act such as walking with a friend for no specific purpose. In rural areas, where there are no paved promenades, the village square takes on the same social function. In the early summer evening, when people have refreshed themselves after a *siesta*, the pavement corners around the square and the outdoor tables of cafés become gathering points for exchanging news.

SOCCER

The most popular sport in Malta is soccer. The game was first introduced to the country by the British, and the tremendous popularity of the sport across Europe, especially in nearby Italy, has assured it of its place in Maltese culture. In most countries, soccer clubs compete with one another in different leagues, according to their level of ability, but because Malta has such a small population the same small number of teams tend to achieve success each year.

PARK LIFE

The municipal park is a familiar part of urban life and nowhere is this more true than in Malta, especially on the weekends. Malta's relaxed and unhurried pace of life, combined with the strong role of the family in most people's lives, help to make the public park a microcosm of national life.

One of the biggest parks is Buskett Gardens near Rabat, with its large wooded grounds. It was designed by Gerolamo Cassar in the late 16th century and was once part of the official summer residence of the British governor. Except in the winter, it is popular with picnicking families and young couples. Every year at the end of June the park is the site of a popular festival.

The limited pool of talent also affects Malta's ability to form an international team capable of competing effectively with other national teams in Europe and North Africa. Although Malta rarely achieves international success, this has not diminished the people's enormous interest in soccer. As it is possible to receive Italian television programs, Italian league games, generally representing some of the most skillful soccer in the world, can be seen in the homes of ordinary Maltese.

Satellite television also offers live English soccer games. A regular Maltese soccer enthusiast is as familiar with top clubs such as Manchester United from England and Juventus from Italy as would be supporters in those countries.

Maltese families enjoying a day at a waterpark.

OTHER SPORTS

Water-based sports such as swimming, water polo, water-skiing, windsurfing, and sailing are also popular with the Maltese. Most of the country's land-based sports, apart from soccer, take place at the Marsa. This large flat area was where the Turks set up base during the Great Siege of 1565. It is now the site of the country's major sports club and where Malta's second most-popular sport, horse-racing, takes place.

Between October and May, weekly race meetings, including trotting races, are held. Trotting races—short and fast races using a pony (a smaller breed of horse) or even a donkey, harnessed to a small, compact vehicle called a sulky—are enormously popular and many Maltese bet on them. Maltese teenagers prefer to spend their leisure time at the large ten-pin bowling alley and roller rink complex on Malta island.

Fishing is popular with men, although it is enjoyed more as a form of relaxation than as an active sport. As a fishing license is not required, the activity is popular with casual fishermen. The rods used are unusually long

because the best fish do not swim close to the shore. Enthusiasts have to clamber out onto the edges of rocky points to get as far out to the sea as possible.

Other sports enjoyed by the Maltese include horse-riding, golf, tennis, squash, badminton, field hockey, basketball, polo, and archery. Golf in Malta dates back to 1888, when the game was introduced by the British governor. Polo is a stick-and-ball game played on horseback by two teams of four. Points are scored by hitting the ball with a hand-held mallet into the opposing team's goal, and each game is divided into a series of seven-minute periods known as chukkas. The game has its origins in central Asia. The water-based version, water polo, was developed by the British in the 19th century and is played in swimming pools. Both sports were introduced into Malta by the British.

KILLING FIELDS

A leisure activity in Malta that most outsiders find difficult to comprehend is the pastime of killing birds. About 5% of the population, mostly men, look forward each year to spring and autumn when they can gather in fields, public parks, and other places to shoot as many small birds as they can. Sparrows, finches, song birds, and up to 100,000 birds of prey, including over 30,000 kestrels, become victims in the mass slaughters that take place annually. It has been estimated that 10 million cartridges are fired each year.

Enthusiasts defend this unusual pastime as an ancient tradition in Malta. Not all Maltese, however, accept this argument. In the late 1990s, a book on the subject written by a Maltese conservationist was published: *Fatal Flight—The Maltese Obsession with Killing Birds*. In it the author pointed out that when Malta becomes a member nation of the European Union it will no longer be able to condone this practice of bird-killing.

Keeping small birds in cages is also a popular Maltese practice. Most street markets have at least one stall selling tiny finches in cages.

The Malta Marathon, first held in 1986, has become an established annual event for the Maltese as well as hundreds of runners from around the world.

THE GAMBLING PASSION

Betting is a national pastime and takes various forms, the most popular being lotteries. A familiar sight in any town is a small trestle table and a vendor holding a roll of lottery tickets for sale. At the most local level a lottery prize may be only a household item, with the profits going to the village fund to finance the annual festival. Some prizes, however, can be very substantial and the results are published in the newspapers and broadcast on television. Gambling also takes the form of local bingo sessions, held in a hall or movie theater, while more serious gamblers can patronize Malta's casino.

FESTIVALS

MALTA'S CAPACITY FOR ENJOYING FESTIVE OCCASIONS is most apparent in the plethora of *festi* ("FEST-e") that punctuate the social calendar between May and September. The *festa* ("FEST-a"), or feast, has its origins in the religious traditions of village communities. The setting aside of at least one day each year to honor the village church's patron saint has become the occasion for each village and town to celebrate its own sense of communal identity.

FESTI

Preparing for a village *festa* is often a hectic activity because of the competition among neighboring villages to mount a more colorful and

Opposite and left: **The country's many festivals are celebrated with a great deal of enthusiasm by the Maltese.**

more exciting event. *Festa* events are scheduled well in advance and are meticulously planned to ensure that everything runs smoothly.

Celebrations take place over at least one weekend and apart from the solemn church services and religious processions, there are numerous secular events that lend a nonreligious flavor to every *festa*. Indeed, for a growing number of Maltese, a visit to the church to appreciate the displays and ornamentation may be the only time in the year that they step inside their local church. The social and festive nature of the *festa* is reflected in the tremendous noise that accompanies such festivals, with every village announcing the imminent arrival of their festival by setting off fireworks.

The notion behind these pre-*festa* celebrations seems to be that the louder the noise, the more confidence the villagers have that their *festa* will be more glamorous than the previous year and more successful and popular than their neighboring village's event. Complementing the noise is the display of multicolored fireworks exploding across the sky. The drama is heightened by the thousands of small colored bulbs strung across streets and hung from public and private buildings.

A highlight of the festival is the processional march of a band, followed by a crowd of local people enjoying the atmosphere. The occasion is a unique blend of the formal and the informal because the musicians make impromptu stops along the way, pausing for complimentary refreshments. The climax takes place on Sunday when the statue of the patron saint is

Festi are noisy, exuberant affairs and a big tourist draw.

paraded through the streets, confetti is thrown from the windows of houses along the route, and a multitude of fireworks light up the sky. At the end of the day, when the streets are empty, it can appear as if there has been a sudden downpour of colored snow because the pavements are literally carpeted in confetti.

Malta's fireworks displays are said to be among the finest to be seen anywhere in Europe.

HISTORY OF THE *FESTA*

The origins of the *festa* go back to the 16th century when the local nobility would play the part of the honorable patron. Once a year the local landowner would finance a small celebration to gain the goodwill of the peasants. Over time, a sense of competition gradually developed between the landowners as some of them used the celebrations to display their generosity and power. Gifts of money to the local church were used to finance the purchase of a statue of the patron saint. The combined influence of the nobility and the Church gradually involved the peasants more and more.

By the early 18th century, a form of fireworks was used for the first time. A decisive factor in the development of the festival was the growing involvement of the Knights as the Order of St. John recognized the value of the celebrations in raising the morale of the poor. It was the wealth of the Order that transformed these minor festivals into spectacular events. Then the British arrived on the scene with their military bands and pomp and ceremony. They encouraged villages to form their own bands because they too saw the value of helping the peasants forget their poverty for at least a few days.

Today, the organization and financing of village festivals is managed completely at the local level. There is no government subsidy. The rich still play a significant role in financing the celebrations and often donate lavish bouquets of flowers for decorating the statue of the patron saint.

Colorful and beautifully decorated floats have become one of the main attractions of Carnival.

CARNIVAL

This was once a religious festival that preceded the first day of Lent, traditionally a period of fasting that leads up to Easter. The beginnings of this Maltese festival, however, go back much further than Christianity and has its origins in a pagan celebration to mark the end of winter. The highlight of this week-long event is a procession of colorful floats that sets off just outside Valletta and makes its way through the gates of the city and into the capital. Some of the more artistic floats take the form of giant displays of flowers carefully laid out on the back of an open truck. Even more time-consuming to design and make are the striking costumes that appear in the parade.

Around the same time of year, the island of Gozo holds a similar festive event, and although it is held on a much smaller scale, it shares with the Valletta festival historical roots based on a primitive celebration of the approach of spring.

BAND CLUBS

It would be difficult to imagine a Maltese festival that did not include the presence of a brass band. Their significance to the national culture has been recognized by the government, which plans to promote their popularity so that they do not die out like other cultural traditions. Band clubs have also been recognized as a useful way to encourage a love of music among the young.

Malta has more than 80 bands, including a police band. The various bands attract about 3,000 musicians of all ages, and many of the residents of each locality are involved in some way with their local band club. The oldest band clubs can trace their history back to the late 19th century. In 1999 the St. Philip band club of Zebbug ("ZE-booje") triumphantly announced that documents had been found proving their band was set up in 1851.

MNARJA

The feast of St. Peter and St. Paul on June 29 is a public holiday and the occasion for an important festival traditionally known as Mnarja ("im-NAAR-ya"), from a Maltese word meaning "light." Its origins are lost in time, but it may have been a country folk festival that has survived into modern times. The traditional start to the festival occurs some days before the event with a formal procession of Boy Scouts from the city of Mdina, accompanied by a band and members of the organizing committee, who carry and display the prizes that will later be awarded to winners of the horse races that will take place June 29.

On the eve of the 29th, the festivities move to Buskett Gardens on the outskirts of Rabat, where an agricultural show is already bustling with activity. Some people will spend the night in the gardens, camping under the trees, and the sound of bands and Spanish guitars is heard until the early hours of the morning.

On the day of the 29th, attention switches back to Mdina, where traditional horse and donkey races take place. An amusing feature of these races is that the animals are ridden bareback and the jockeys have to grip their mounts with their knees, while driving the animals forward with a short stick. In the 17th and 18th centuries, special races were held for slaves until they were abolished by Napoleon in 1798. After the races the prizes are distributed, an ancient tradition that goes back at least three centuries, according to a Latin motto inscribed on the walls of the city: *Cuicumque legitime certaverit* ("For all who lawfully strive to win").

CHRISTMAS

Unlike the celebrations in many other European countries, Christmas in Malta is far less of a public festival and much less commercial in spirit. This is mainly because of the traditional religious significance that is still attached to Christmas. Familiar practices include the decorating of streets and buildings with colored lights and community groups singing carols in public places. Christmas trees are also decorated and placed in the windows of homes and gifts are exchanged between friends and family members, but there is little of the shopping frenzy seen in some European cities in the weeks and days leading up to Christmas.

December 25 is essentially a family celebration. Shops and businesses all close. One of the busiest places is the arrival hall of Malta's only international airport as many Maltese working and living abroad return home to be with their families.

During festivities, the church is often ornamented with thousands of colored light bulbs so that it becomes the most prominent structure at night.

A vendor sells palm leaves during Holy Week.

HOLY WEEK

Holy Week marks the religious celebrations leading to Easter Sunday. Compared to most other festive occasions it is a somber event, commemorating the death and resurrection of Christ. It starts on the Friday of the week before the Easter weekend with a major procession through the streets of Valletta and smaller processions in other towns.

On the following Thursday, traditional "Last Supper" displays are held in religious institutions in some towns, commemorating the last meal of Christ and his apostles, as described in the New Testament of the Bible. A traditional display features a table prepared for Christ and his 12 apostles with fresh loaves, wine-jars, and pastries.

The next day is Good Friday, the day that traditionally marks the crucifixion of Christ. Good Friday is a public holiday and all businesses and entertainment outlets are closed. Processions with life-sized statues depicting scenes associated with the biblical event take place in many towns.

Easter Sunday is a day of celebration, marking the Christian belief that on this day Christ was resurrected. Like Christmas Day, this is very much a family occasion. Relatives and friends visit one another's houses, and Easter eggs are presented to children. A special sweet, the *figolla* ("FIG-ole-ar"), a pastry cut into various shapes such as the Maltese Cross, is prepared for this day. It is filled with marzipan and covered with colored icing.

PUBLIC HOLIDAYS

Many of Malta's public holidays mark religious events. The few exceptions either celebrate nationalist events or commemorate workers' rights:

January 1	New Year's Day
February 10	St. Paul's Shipwreck
March 19	St. Joseph's Day
March 31	Freedom Day
April	Good Friday
May 1	Workers' Day
June 7	Commemoration of 1919 Riot
August 15	The Assumption of Our Lady into Heaven
September 8	Great Siege of Victories (Our Lady of Victories)
September 21	Independence Day
December 8	Feast of the Immaculate Conception
December 13	Republic Day
December 25	Christmas Day

FOOD

MALTESE FOOD, LIKE ITS HISTORY, owes much to various foreign cultures. Obvious examples of this are pasta, introduced from Italy, and British fare such as fish and chips. The first appearance of British food may have its origins in colonial history, but the annual invasion by hundreds of thousands of vacationers from Britain has helped popularize some of these dishes in restaurants and, indirectly, in the homes of Maltese families.

Many of the more fashionable restaurants in Malta today are influenced by Italian or French cuisine. However, Malta also has a distinctive Maltese cuisine that, like its language, has managed to survive and prosper, despite centuries of foreign domination.

Opposite and left: **The Maltese have developed their own form of cuisine over the years, based on basic, nourishing cooking.**

A café in Valletta. Businessmen often pick a regular café as a meeting place.

MALTESE FOOD

Maltese food is the product of a rural society, but the country's climate and ecology has also made a significant contribution. Many vegetables can be grown throughout the year and are readily available to all families. The scarcity of firewood for ovens in the days when electricity or gas was not commonly available accounts for the tradition of cooking food slowly in earthenware pots.

In the past it was not unusual to take food to the village baker to be roasted in his oven after the bread had been taken out for the day. Although modern technology has eliminated the need to do this, this style of cooking continues to influence the nature and taste of traditional dishes. Even the tradition of taking food to the baker has not died out completely—on Sundays this can still be observed in some villages in Gozo.

A café in Valletta. Businessmen often pick a regular café as a meeting place.

116

A rural lifestyle and the fact that in the past the majority of Maltese were not well-off also accounts for the popularity of soups. Because the vegetables are grown locally, a glut of some types of vegetables occurs now and then. This reduces their price and encourages people to combine their flavors over slow cooking. *Minestra* ("MIN-ess-traa"), a type of minestrone, is often prepared for lunch or as a first course for an evening meal, but depending on the quantity and type of ingredients, it can easily become a filling meal in itself.

Another vegetable dish is *soppa tal armla* ("SOP-pah taal AM-laa"), which is quite different in character and taste from the bulky and chunky *minestra*. Instead of using thick portions of six to 10 different ingredients, *soppa tal armla* uses only white and green vegetables and is traditionally served with goat cheese. *Aljotta* ("AL-yacht-ta"), a light broth made from fish, is especially popular in the summer months when fish is plentiful.

Yet another traditional vegetable soup is kusksu *("kus-KSUE"), made from broad beans with pasta and tomatoes.*

A fish vendor in Mar-saxlokk keeps her fish fresh.

NATIONAL DISHES

Fenek ("fe-NECK"), or rabbit, is one of Malta's most popular and distinctive dishes. It is eaten stewed, roasted, or fried. The origins of this dish are not difficult to understand for when families were poor and food was scarce, it was always possible to hunt or trap a rabbit. Nowadays, wild rabbits may no longer be abundant in the countryside, but the popularity of rabbit as a dish has not diminished and they are reared specially for the kitchen.

Another national dish is *lampuka* ("lam-POO-ka"), which is actually a seasonal swordfish called the *dorado* ("door-add-o"). The fish is relatively easy for local fishermen to catch with nets. The swordfish is fried or baked in a pie with olives, cauliflower, spinach, chestnuts, and raisins. Almost as popular is *bragioli* ("BRA-geo-lee"), tiny parcels of stuffing wrapped in slices of beef and cooked slowly at low temperature.

MALTESE BREAD

The mass-produced bread that is sold in supermarkets is a far cry from the traditional Maltese bread. Sour-dough Maltese bread is baked on the surface of an oven that gives it a firm crust but with a soft, light center. The customary way to eat the bread is by adding olive oil, hence its name *hobz biz-zejt* ("hops BIZ-zeyt"), which translates simply as "bread with oil." Tomatoes are first rubbed onto a slice of the bread, coloring it naturally. Peppers and capers are then added, before finally pouring on the olive oil.

Stewed rabbit is a great favorite with the Maltese.

FAST FOOD

Fast food has found its way to Malta and does not just cater to tourists. In fashionable areas such as Sliema, numerous small restaurants serve burgers, pizza, and Chinese food in plastic containers. An American fast-food chain that first opened in Valletta in 1995 now has an outlet for every 45,000 people, giving Malta the highest market penetration in the world outside of the United States.

But Malta had its own local fast food long before the now familiar franchises first appeared. Known as *pastizzi* ("PAST-TITS-see"), these are flaky pastry snacks with a savory taste best enjoyed when warm and fresh. They are sometimes, mistakenly, translated as cheesecakes because cheese is the most common filling, but they taste little like the sweet North American cheesecake.

Salad with *hobz biz-zejt*. Traditional Maltese bread is a versatile snack as additional tastes can be added by using garlic or herbs.

The Maltese have a sweet tooth, and cakes and biscuits are popular snacks.

PASTA

Maltese families do not eat pasta as frequently as Italians do, but the dish is enormously popular, both in the home and in restaurants. Two of the most popular traditional dishes are baked pasta—*timpana* ("TIM-paa-nah") and *mqarrun fil-forn* ("IM-ah-roon ill-fourn"). Both dishes are made of macaroni with layers of meat, cheese, tomatoes, and eggs, while *timpana* is wrapped in light pastry.

DESSERTS

There are a number of traditional Maltese desserts. Nougat and hot, date-stuffed fried fritters are popular. Another favorite, usually eaten at the end of a meal with tea or coffee, is *kannoli* ("can-ON-lee"), a tube-shaped confection of deep-fried crisp pastry filled with a mixture of fresh whipped cream, small pieces of candied fruit and chocolate, and ricotta cheese. A light dusting of powdered sugar and pistachios complete this delicacy, which originated in Sicily.

DRINKS

It is thought that the Phoenicians first brought the skill of making wine to Malta and that the process was revived in the 17th century by the Knights of St. John. Today, local grapes are used to produce wines that carry floral and fruity flavors. The strongest wines are produced on Gozo by small family enterprises.

The Maltese are not heavy beer drinkers, although there is a popular beer called *Cisk* ("CHISK") that is brewed on the island. There is also a popular non-alcoholic drink called Kinnie, which is made using herbs that give it a distinctive taste. Malta also produces a liquor called *bajtra* ("BITE-trah") from the fruit of the prickly pear cactus. It has a bright pink color and a sweet taste.

A selection of Maltese wines.

ALJOTTA (FISH SOUP)

1 tablespoon olive oil	1 lb (0.45 kg) tomatoes, sliced
2 onions, peeled and chopped	1 lb (0.45 kg) white fish
4 garlic cloves, cut into tiny pieces	1 pint (0.5 liter) fish stock
1/2 teaspoon marjoram	black pepper

Heat the olive oil in a pan. Add the onion, frying gently until soft and turning color. Then add the garlic and marjoram and cook for five minutes. Add the tomatoes, fish, and fish stock and bring to a boil slowly, stirring occasionally.

Add pepper and simmer for 10 minutes. Serve with rice.

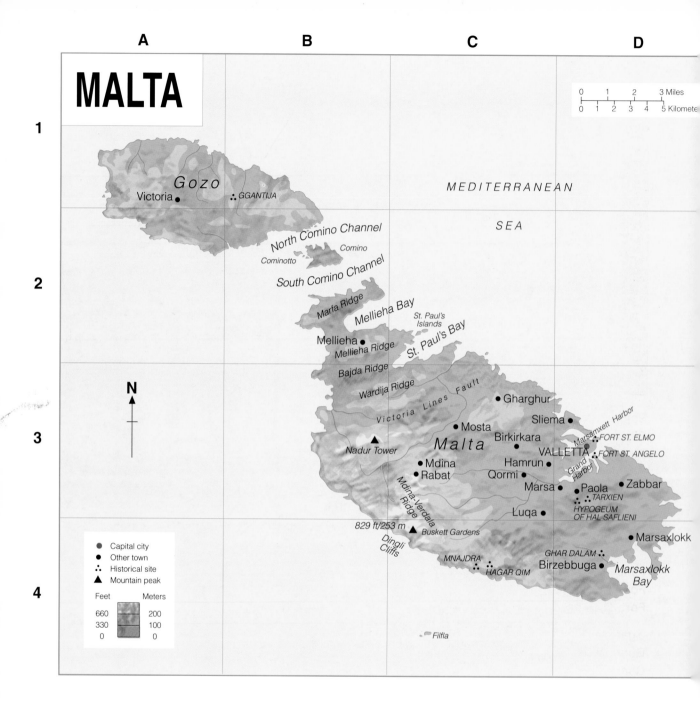

MALTA

Gozo

Victoria •

∴ GGANTIJA

MEDITERRANEAN

SEA

North Comino Channel

Comino

Cominotto

South Comino Channel

Marfa Ridge

Mellieha Bay

St. Paul's
Islands

Mellieha •

Mellieha Ridge

St. Paul's Bay

Bajda Ridge

Wardija Ridge

Victoria Lines Fault

• Gharghur

Sliema •

Marsamxett Harbor

• Mosta

Malta

Birkirkara

•

VALLETTA ∴ FORT ST. ELMO

▲

Nadur Tower

Hamrun

•

∴ FORT ST. ANGELO

• Mdina

Qormi •

*Grand
Harbor*

• Rabat

Marsa •

Paola

∴ Zabbar

∴ TARXIEN

*Mdina-Verdala
Ridge*

Luqa •

HYPOGEUM
OF HAL SAFLIENI

829 ft/253 m ▲ Buskett Gardens

• Marsaxlokk

*Dingli
Cliffs*

MNAJDRA
∴

GHAR DALAM ∴

∴

HAGAR QIM

Birzebbuga •

*Marsaxlokk
Bay*

▨ Filfla

N

0   1   2   3 Miles
0   1   2   3   4   5 Kilometers

●	Capital city
●	Other town
∴	Historical site
▲	Mountain peak

Feet		Meters
660		200
330		100
0		0

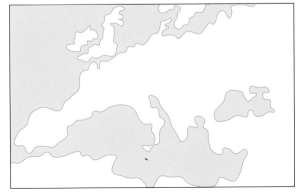

QUICK NOTES

OFFICIAL NAME
Republic of Malta

AREA
122 square miles (316 square km)

POPULATION
375,000 (1997 estimate)

CAPITAL
Valletta

OFFICIAL LANGUAGES
Maltese and English

HIGHEST POINT
Dingli Cliffs (829 feet / 253 m)

MAIN RELIGION
Roman Catholicism

MAIN ISLANDS
Malta, Gozo, Comino

MAJOR TOWNS
Birkirkara, Qormi, Mosta, Zabbar, Sliema

CLIMATE
Mediterranean

NATIONAL FLAG
Two equal vertical stripes, white at the hoist and red at the fly, with a representation of the George Cross, edged with red, in the upper hoist.

CURRENCY
The Maltese lira (LM)
1 lira = 100 cents
US$1 = LM0.39 or 39 cents

MAIN EXPORTS
Machinery and transportation equipment, and manufactured and semimanufactured goods

MAJOR IMPORTS
Manufactured goods, machinery and transportation equipment, fuels, chemicals, foodstuffs

POLITICAL LEADERS
Dominic Mintoff—prime minister, 1955–58 and 1971–84
Eddie Fenech Adami—prime minister, 1987–96, 1998–present

MAIN POLITICAL PARTIES
Malta Labor Party
Nationalist Party

SOME FAMOUS MALTESE
Jean de la Valette (1494–1566), Grand Master of the Order of St. John
Gerolamo Cassar (1520–86), architect
Dun Karm (1871–1961), writer

ANNIVERSARIES
Great Siege Victory (September 8)
Independence Day (September 21)
Republic Day (December 13)

GLOSSARY

aljotta ("AL-yacht-ta")
A light broth made from fish.

auberge ("ou-BERGE")
An inn of residence for the Knights of the Order of St. John.

bragioli ("BRA-geo-lee")
Tiny parcels of stuffing wrapped in slices of beef and cooked slowly at low temperature.

faqqus il-hmir ("FAT-ous ill-hmeer")
Squirting cucumber, an unusual plant whose fruits explode when ripe.

fenek ("fe-NECK")
Rabbit, a popular dish in Malta.

festa ("FEST-a")
Feast.

figolla ("FIG-ole-ar")
A pastry cut into various shapes, such as the Maltese Cross, prepared for Easter Sunday celebrations.

ghana ("ANN-aa")
Poems that are sung to musical accompaniment.

gregale ("grey-GAH-lay")
A cooling wind that blows in from the mountains in Italy.

hobz biz-zejt ("hops BIZ-zeyt")
Maltese bread with olive oil.

karozzin ("ca-rotts-SEEN")
Horse-drawn carriage.

Knights
Members of the Order of St. John, a religious and military group that ruled Malta from 1530–1798.

lampuka ("lam-POO-ka")
A swordfish dish popular with the Maltese.

luzzijiet ("LUT-tsie-yiet")
Traditional Maltese fishing boats.

niccec ("nee-chech")
Contribution boxes placed at shrines to the saints.

pulizija ("PULL-IT-see-ya")
Maltese police force.

scirocco ("shi-ROCK-o")
A warm and sultry wind that blows across Malta from the Sahara at the beginning and end of each summer.

siesta ("see-ES-ta")
Afternoon rest period.

Te Deum ("tay DAY-um")
A hymn of praise sung at a special service on the eve of feast day.

timpana ("TIM-paa-nah")
A traditional pasta-based dish.

BIBLIOGRAPHY

Balm, Roger. *Malta (American Geographical Society Around the World Program)*. McDonald & Woodward Pub Co, 1996.

Levy, Pat. *Essential Malta and Gozo*. Basingstoke, UK: AA Publications, 1998.

Malta: A Guide to the Islands' Heritage. National Tourism Organization of Malta.

Pickles, Tim. *Malta 1565: Last Battle of the Crusades (Campaign, No 50)*. Stackpole Books, 1998.

Seth, Ronald. *Let's Visit Malta*. London: Burke Publishing, 1985.

Shores, Christopher, Cull, Brian & Malizia, Nicola. *Malta: The Spitfire Year, 1942*. Seven Hills Book Distributors, 1991.

Sire, H.J.A. *The Knights of Malta*. New Haven: Yale University Press, 1996.

INDEX

INDEX

INDEX